Murder and Deceit

The Story of Jack Nissalke

John K. Bucher

SIDESHOW MEDIA GROUP
Los Angeles / Austin
www.sideshowmediagroup.com

ISBN 978-097-614658-2

First Edition

10 9 8 7 6 5 4 3 2 1

Manufactured in the United States of America

CONTENTS

For Kristal Nissalke

Introduction

This is a true story. In fact, it's still ongoing. The murder of Ada Senenfelder occurred on June 6, 1985, but my involvement had to wait until the summer of 2009. By sheer luck, I wandered into an old Hollywood bar named Boardners looking for a cold beverage and a new adventure. I had no idea what lay in store. I had recently moved to Hollywood from Colorado and was still awestruck with my new surroundings—and what might lay ahead. After writing several novels, my eldest son convinced me to try and adapt some into screenplays, and the glow of Hollywood Boulevard had begun its seduction.

Boardners has served as the watering hole to the stars since the 1920s. It's an enchanting place and you can feel the magic when you enter past the curtain. As a writer, I seem to thrive best when I have a connection to a coffee shop and a bar. The atmosphere and the people there seem to ground me to real life and keeps my soul churning with new ideas. After my move, I had tried out many places in West Hollywood and a character named CJ I met one day at The Pig and Whistle took me to Boardners and introduced me around. I would not see CJ again for over a year. Somewhere between becoming a frequent customer and a regular, I met a pretty bartender named Kristal Nissalke, who also had just relocated to Hollywood. Being from Minnesota, we held some common interest as I was in the middle of connection with some long lost cousins in that state. After a while, we became friends and she began to tell me and the other regulars of a strange story about her brother. She had just returned from Minnesota and said that her brother had just been convicted of murder. His name was Jack Nissalke, and the court handed him a life sentence. Kristal insisted he was innocent and I became intrigued enough to take a look at the story. At first, I was appalled at what the newspapers said. This was a Manson-type killing with the victim being stabbed over 30 times. The consensus was that a cold-blooded killer got what he deserved.

Something bothered me. How could she be so sure Jack was innocent? Was it family love? I couldn't imagine being protective of a family member if they had killed somebody. I would be ashamed, guilty over it. I took another look. I didn't have much information and asked Kristal for Jack's address. I began a conversation with a man I did not know. What came back to my mailbox was unexpected. His letters were long and detailed. He answered all my questions, even the hard ones, and I would write again. I only had a small amount of evidence, but one thing was clear—Jack couldn't have done it. Down the road, as I would later discuss this with strangers, their eyes would roll and tune me out. People would look at me in amazement as if I was telling them that secretly I could fly. Usually if people gave me three minutes I could outline this very complex tale. I knew I needed more evidence, at his trial the judge would not allow volumes of key evidence and I sought to get my hands on it. I wrote dozens of letters. At first no one wanted to talk to me or help, outside Jack's family. Jack's dad, Ron began to share with me all he had, and that was quite a bit. I couldn't believe the hundreds of documents this man had gathered. My journey began to get deeper and so did my obsession.

Fiction writing comes naturally to me. This type does not, and I had to learn again. My heart told me I was the "one" to do this story and I felt the pressure of knowing a man's fate may hang in the balance. With each letter, I felt a connection with Jack, as one would with a brother or relative. I would rise at 4:00 a.m. and reread his letters. Gradually, my life was changed. Josh Bucher, son number 3, urged me start a blog. With in a month I had hundreds of readers, which has become thousands. With it came detractors. The Winona legal system was in the spotlight in a negative way and I was making enemies. After my daily intake of beer and friendship, I no longer cared. My lust for the Hollywood lifestyle began to pale as I only wanted to tell this story and free this man. I became possessed.

In June, 2010, John Jr., son number 1, and I traveled to Minnesota. I had done months of prep work before we went, and felt I was trying to do too much. The first leg of the trip was to reconnect with three of my cousins (all female, all nurses) and visit my father's home town. I had not been there since I was a baby. Ironic, all this was in Minnesota, right? The experience was wonderful as I saw the beauty of the state. I walked around a hillside cemetery, "land where my fathers died". Finally seeing, Betty, Bronwyn, and Sally resolved many personal issues.

The second half of the trip found us in a hurry to get to Winona. My heart pounded when we saw the city limit sign. John Jr. and I went to meet Ron, Bonnie, Laurie, and Julie Nissalke. Ron greeted us at the door and they family gave us a warm welcome. For hours we sat at their dinning room table and talked about Jack's plight. I was struck by the reality of this story by looking into their eyes. Later we met Sarah Elmquist, a reporter from *The Winona Post*. She has been invaluable to me and helped make this book happen. Sarah pointed out the original crime scene and took pictures of us in front of Ada's house. It would end up on the front of the Sunday paper. Sarah is a great writer as we have become friends. Winona is a beautiful city and my life and future have become entwined with it.

John Jr. and I met with an investigator that was gracious and helpful to provide me the hard evidence I needed to show the world, beyond any doubt, that Jack Nissalke is innocent. Most of this was never presented to the jury. It's a long drive up to prison in Rush City, where Jack is confined. Later in the book, I will take you there. Jack is a wonderful, sweet man that has become a brother to me. I want you to know what an unlikely story this is, but is becoming more likely every day. However, this is not a story—this is real.

June 5, 1985

On a warm Wednesday evening on June 5, 1985, Ada Senenfelder ate a simple meal of meatloaf, corn from a can, and mashed potatoes, at the home of Van Lear Daniels with Van Lear and Bonnie Fegre. After thanking them, she mounted her 15 speed bike and rode home about 5:30 p.m.. Ada seemed worried about something, but didn't say what it might be. As this was her last meal, Ada had plenty to worry about. That night, her house seemed busy, even though she was living by herself at the time. Ada, a mother of five, had numerous problems being a fit mother and all five kids were in foster care. They had been in and out of foster care for the past two years. The month before, Scott Boss, with Social Services had signed an order permanently removing them from her care. That night, three different men were held in jail, on her sole testimony. One of them was about to get even.

Several neighbors noticed the car traffic in and out of the street. They were used to her parties and the stream of strangers that came and went. What concerned them most was when her children were there. They would knock on their doors, hungry and frightened. William Bartz, her next door neighbor, watched Magnum P.I. and heard loud voices at her door and saw a brown car in the street. He and several others noticed Ada flicking her porch light on and off repeatedly and wondered if she was all right. No one bothered to check. Bartz was awakened again at 2:30 am by loud talking. He went back to sleep.

In the morning a neighbor, Mike Paskiewicz, was walking his dog when he saw what looked liked Ada lying against the window, tangled up in the curtains between the bed and the wall. She looked sick. Mike and his wife had seen that her TV had been on all night as their house in only a few feet from hers. Later, about 10 am, she was still in the same position. He went over and saw her through the window, covered in blood. He ran to phone the police at the Bartz house. The Winona Police arrived quickly and taped off the block. Members of the Bureau of Criminal Apprehension were notified and they came in their white lab coats. For the next eight hours, they gathered evidence in her little house. The news went out all over Winona, Ada Senenfelder, age 40, was dead, brutally stabbed over 30 times with a knife.

The *Winona Daily News* would describe it as a mystery the next day. They would go on to mention that Ada Frances Senenfelder had put a criminal in jail, one Bobby Fort.

The following day, the paper would report it as an open homicide and the investigation was ongoing. By June 12, the police had interviewed 12 people, among them, Jack Nissalke, Linda Parrish, Ed Bolstad, Jimmy Bolstad, and Rena Bambenek. Search warrants were forth coming and the Chief was tight lipped about any possible suspects. The investigation was exhaustive and thorough. However, for some reason, nothing transpired that seemed to solve the case. The headlines soon told a fruitless tale: June 9, NO NEW DEVELOPMENTS ON SENENFELDER CASE, June 18, NO NEW EVIDENCE IN SENENFELDER CASE, June 21, POLICE LACK KEY EVIDENCE IN MURDER CASE, each article getting smaller and deeper in the back pages. The year of 1985 would end with no arrests and no new developments. Most murders, actually crimes in general, are solved in the 3 day period after the crime was committed. They had all they would ever get, however they had enough to solve it. In 1986, the police continued to interview the same people over and over. There seemed to be multiple motives to kill Ada. The police seemed confused but still amassed quite a volume of paperwork. This continued over the next 20 years. They never got a single break, but continued to talk to people who would suddenly remember something. Most of the interviewees were in and out of jail, and would gladly talk about the case for any consideration in a reduction of their sentence.

By 2006, Winona County had shelves and shelves of paperwork, all labeled ADA SENENFELDER – HOMICIDE. This had now become the county's only unsolved homicide, and the County Attorney, Charles 'Chuck' MacLean decided it was finally time to close this embarrassing chapter, and bring some sort of justice to this brutal murder. County Attorneys are elected and you can win them by this sort of 'Law and Order', 'Cold Case', trials. This would prove to be a daunting task. Much of the crime scene evidence was now missing, gone. Many of the prime suspects were all dead, some mysteriously. Most of the ones who gave testimony over and over were of questionable character and would change their stories dramatically. 1985 was a long time ago and memories do not age like wine. Still, MacLean was determined to have this on his resume. He made a wanted poster.

The poster declared *Up to $50,000 Reward.* He stated that the evidence was now being re-examined, and with new DNA techniques, solving the crime was now possible. He just needs a little help. MacLean had convinced the BCA (Bureau of Criminal Apprehension) to get Spotlight on Crime (A citizens' group) to cough up this very large amount of cash. By the summer of 2009, MacLean was smiling. He and his Assistant, a fellow named Tom Gort had a jury conviction of one Jack Willis Nissalke. Case closed. Or was it? This is the story of how an innocent man received a life sentence by a broken system and deceitful people. Please let me introduce you to all these folks. I hope it breaks your heart as it has mine.

Who Was Ada Senenfelder?

Ada Frances Senenfelder's life was a complicated journey with many a dark turn. She was raised in a rough environment where sex with men, and bars were a fact of life at an early age. She married Casmir Flak and had three children, Helen, Tim, and Mary. When Casmir died of cancer in 1978, she quickly remarried a man named John Senenfelder. They had two more children, Peggy and Jenny. John was a plumber and made good money. They bought a small cottage at 566 E. Fourth Street in Winona. After a few years, Ada filed charges against her husband and had him arrested. The charge? She claimed he was having sex with his stepdaughter, Helen. John was sentenced to a little over four years in prison. Ada was free to party and live a single life again, and wasted no time doing so. She neglected her children and Social Services were called in. What they found was deplorable. Upon the first house visit, they found decay, and the smell of urine. Piles of trash and moldy food was everywhere. The shower stall had a 20 gallon trash can that was full. There was no where to even lay down in the house except small areas of the floor. The children were in bad shape. The girls all were dirty with red sores in on their genitals. Tim was found to have disabilities that included a speech impediment and mild retardation. Ada, herself only had an IQ of 87. Tim, besides other problems, had head lice. The children were swiftly placed into foster care and the foster parents reported how difficult the task was. The younger children did not know how to brush their teeth or get between the sheets at bed time. All reported being slapped around and called names. Tim said his mother would put a dress on him and mock him. They wet the bed and needed constant supervision. They were all malnourished and needed human contact night and day.

The year before Ada was murdered, Social Services contacted her over 130 times. A pattern soon developed. Ada would clean up her house. She shopped for groceries on her bicycle. She would beg to have her children returned, and they were. Soon, the neighbors would complain to Social Services that the kids were on their door step, hungry and dirty. Off they would go to a home with heat to guard against the hard Minnesota winters. Ada would beg to have them returned. Some or all would be taken back to the home on Fourth Street. The cycle came to a halt in May, 1985, when Scott Boss would sign the order to have all 5 permanently removed. Ada had been hosting large parties that involved kinky sex, even her having sex with a pit bull before teen boys. A month later, she would be dead, and the children damaged for life.

The summer of 1984, Ada moved in with Bobby Fort. This was the beginning of a series of mistakes that would cost her life. Clyde Dewaine "Bobby" Fort was a fence. The dictionary has several meanings, and the one I mean is a "dealer in stolen goods." Bobby was a true river man making his life off the Mississippi. At age 66, he still loved to hunt, trap and fish. He had never had a conventional job, as the river supplied him with all he needed. In his basement, he had racks of furs taken from mink, muskrat, and raccoon. He had a freezer that was full of furs freshly bought and ready for processing. He had a large supply of river fish he smoked and sold. The most profitable segment of his river business was his ability to attract teen boys to steal practically anything and bring it to him at night. They prowled the river at night for boat motors, power tools, chain saws, and guns. As soon as they delivered the stolen goods, Bobby would reach into his pocket and pull out a roll and peel off large bills. A chain saw would bring $75, while a boat motor would cash out a $150 to $200. This was the early 1980's and Bobby Fort paid way better that some of the Winona factories or truck driving.

Bobby was smart. He and a Wisconsin man, Earl Lemon, employed only underage males to steal, and usually kept their hands clean. If one of them ever got busted, juvenile hall was the punishment, not prison. Bobby had a brown station wagon, and used different boys to take the goods over the bridge into the waiting buyers he knew along the route to Chicago.

Ada moved her freezer from her house on Fourth Street down to Bobby's basement to expand the room for the furs. She became the queen of the house and loved her new found surroundings. Her children would visit and sometimes sexual advances were made toward them by Fort and the others. Ada never discouraged this kind of behavior. She would walk around the house nude and began to answer the door that way. Ada's friends would visit as she would take them to the bedroom and proudly show them the pile of guns there. Bobby would get her to perform sex acts for his friends, and she seemed to enjoy the new-found attention. She also began to be possessive of Fort and the house. She paid attention to the fencing operation and received money from it. When Bobby's young friends would report with stolen goods to sell, she would answer the door, "that fucking kid's here again." To which Bobby would answer, "Well let him in."

The day Bobby Fort always feared came one day. Larry Kukowski, one of the teen age driver got caught across the river in Wisconsin. He was unprepared to be grilled by the FBI, the ATF, and the Bureau of Criminal Apprehension, in addition to the local police in Wisconsin and Minnesota. He confessed to everything. To verify his statements, the authorities paid a visit to Ada Senenfelder. She had been an informant for them before and they were delighted to find she was actually living with Fort. Ada gladly verified Larry's story and gave them 16 pages of testimony. In November of 1984, they arrested Clyde Dwaine "Bobby" Fort, and Earl Lemon. This sent a shock wave from Winona, all the way up the fencing pipeline. A lot of people were reading the paper and getting sick at their stomach. Fort and Lemon asked for court appointed counsel. They convinced the court they couldn't afford one, and even in light of the proof they were rolling in cash from stolen guns and other goods, the judge granted their request. The taxpayer got a raw deal this time. In January of 1985, Judge Dennis Challeen sentenced Larry Kukowski to the juvenile prison in Red Wing. Over in Wisconsin, Paul Wieczorek, 18, was sentenced to 90 days in jail. In another court room in Winona, Bobby Fort received 150 days in county jail and 5 years probation. Earl Lemon got a 10 day jail term and 3 years probation. Both men could have received a 5 year state prison sentence. It's another mystery why they got such light sentences. The newspaper had a foot note at the end of the article, though. The Federal Bureau of Alcohol, Tobacco, and Firearms was drawing up Federal gun charges. When Bobby's 5 month jail sentence was over, the hard truth was clear. He would plead guilty to a Federal crime and at age 67, probably die in prison. This would transpire based on Ada's co-operation. Bobby was terrified of dying in prison. He needed a friend. He needed Ed Bolstad.

The same day Fort pled guilty, Ed Bolstad entered a not guilty plea for the charge of stabbing a night club bouncer. Edward John Bolstad, 32, was drunk one night at the Country Connection. He fell off a bar stool and took out a knife. Witnesses saw him stab Richard Lynn. When the police arrested Ed, he cried "I hope I stabbed the fucker!" Oddly enough, a Winona jury would find him 'not guilty', a few days after Ada was found dead. Even more odd was that Ken Warzecha, Bobby Fort's close associate and sometimes house guest, pled guilty to scuffling with the police as they arrested Bolstad.

By this time, Ada found herself back at home and back to having to worry about feeding her kids, back in her care. She also found the waiting arm of the Bolstad family. She was friendly with Adeline, the mother of James, Roger, Edward, Albert and June. The Bolstad family were working class people who were constantly at odds with the police. They loved to party and Ada needed a new circle to keep her company. Over a few months, she turned into a willing servant for them. Ada began to frequent Jim Bolstad's apartment where parties happened every night. Ada would clean the place up after the party was over, supply food, buy beer, and have sex with most of the partygoers.

Over most of this year, Ada has been an enigma to me. I have tried to understand who she was, how she lived, and why she died. I think I have tried as hard as anyone ever has to understand her. I have come closer but failed. She had come to a place in life where she was totally unfit as a mother, partied every night and was taking risks that were increasingly dangerous. That description fits many people who don't end up dead. The other habit Ada acquired was to play both sides of life. She had sex with criminals. She loved their lifestyle. Then she would ride her bicycle to the Law Enforcement Center and give pages of testimony that would result in a prison sentence. Later she would be amazed how pissed they would be. I have discussed her actions with many learned folk and some think that Ada would have moments of clarity where she would be reaching out for help. She would beg Social Services to remove her children. She would tell the police the crimes she encountered. She knew right from wrong. Others can not get past the abuse her children suffered, the sex parties, the sex with a dog, the feeding of the Bolstads, and her children who went hungry. Ada, with her 87 IQ, will always be an enigma to me. I have nearly gone insane looking at the many pictures of her dead eyes and bloody body. I have had nightmares where she cries out to me, to find her killers and solve this case. Who is Ada Frances Senenfelder? I still can't answer that, even after talking to her husband John for several days.

Who Is Jack Willis Nissalke?

After the last chapter, this is a much easier question to answer. When I first became interested in this story, I got Jack's address from Kristal and wrote him a letter. She had already told him about me and my interest, so when he received my first letter, he was ready and wrote be promptly and surprised me in several ways. The way he wrote and the clarity of his mind intrigued me in a way I did not expect. I sat down and made a list of very hard questions, licked the envelope and mailed it to Rush City prison. In about a week, I held a 22 page tome that not only answered all my questions, but was sentenced in a sound and intelligent manner. I felt comfortable with Jack and he seemed to have a good heart. He included a large chart from his trial with all the people involved pictures and connections to each other. I began to understand a very complicated tale that was over 20 years old. Our letters to each other were frequent and somewhere along the way, we became friends and brothers. Through pure evidence, not a feeling, I became 100% sure Jack couldn't have done this. In preparation for my first trip to visit Winona and Rush City, Jack and I filled out endless forms back and forth as he agreed to release all the files his attorney and investigator held. I was approved to visit, along with my oldest son, John Jr. When we walked into the maximum-security facility that is Jack's cruel home, we were nervous and unaware how this first meeting with a man I already knew would feel. After a long wait, and endless sets of locks, we stood face-to-face. For more than three hours, the three of us talked about a range of subjects—mainly his case and the current state of the legal proceedings. We posed for pictures and left. Back in the car, I began to sob as my son comforted me. I couldn't bear to leave Jack there, so far from his family and the ones who loved him. Who is Jack Nissalke? I can answer that easily.

Jack is a big fellow, who matured into his large frame by the 7th grade. Jack was always popular with the girls and was taught the love of racing by his father, Ron. As he grew into his teen years, Jack experimented with drugs and alcohol. He soon ran into trouble and was court ordered into a treatment facility. There he met Shelly Stoeckly, and they began to date. They soon moved in with Jack's parents and siblings, Laurie and Kristal. Because of his size, Jack could get into bars at an early age. As he and Shelly resumed partying at the local watering holes, they found the company of the Bolstads. Jack soon caught the eye of June Bolstad and Shelly had to move back to her parents. The Bolstads had a nightly party at their house, and by this time Jack had reached 18. He would join June with her brothers, and a host of friends who would chip in for the nightly beer, whisky and pot. Soon, the Bolstads met Linda Parrish, who was newly widowed, and was flush with her husband's life insurance. The party soon drifted more and more to Linda's apartment. Jack and June soon moved in with Linda and no longer worked at their jobs any more. Linda had begun to date Jim Bolstad, and Jack's sister, Laurie who was 17, was dating Roger Bolstad. These kids were in heaven, to get to party and socialize when ever they wanted to. One night at a party at Jim Bolstad's apartment, Ada Senenfelder showed up. She, too would contribute to the fun, by bringing food and cash. Jim's neighbor, Rena Bambenek, would come over frequently and was fond of Ed Bolstad. A host of others learned of these parties, and soon a crowd would gather nightly to enjoy. The Bolstads made a living dealing drugs and selling stolen goods to Bobby Fort. Everything was pretty nice, until Ada showed up. Ada began to use her sexual appetite to work her way into the partygoers. She began to have sex with Ed Bolstad, much to Rena's dismay. Rena even caught them in bed together. Ada had sex with Jim, which frustrated Linda. Ada offered herself and her daughter, Helen, to the underage kids coming to the parties. With her husband in

Murder and Deceit

prison, Bobby Fort in jail, she felt free to do anything she wanted. Jack met her a few times and felt creeped out by her. Ada was not a pretty woman, and Jack never saw the attraction to sleep with her as the others were.

Finally, Ada went to the police and accused Jim Bolstad of molesting her daughter, Helen, 16 at the time, and Jim was arrested. Jim, on probation at the time, was now in a position now to be revoked and sent to prison. To Ada's surprise, she was no longer welcome at the Bolstad-Parrish parties, and felt confused. Several of the partygoers felt she had lied about Jim, and asked her to recant. She agreed. We don't know if it was to tell the truth, or to get back in the party. On June 5, 1985, Linda, Jack, and June, met Jim's probation officer at Ada's house while she gave a signed, written statement recanting that Helen was molested by Jim Bolstad. Interestingly enough, in her original statement, she confessed to orchestrating the sex between Jim and Helen, yet no one thought to arrest her. The probation officer sadly told them that Jim was going to prison anyway.

The same afternoon, Jack went home to his parents' house as Ron and Bonnie had purchased a new Weber Grill and were cooking supper. After supper, he and June went to Linda's to drink and party with several others. During the party, Ed Bolstad would leave and not return for several hours. The police showed up from a loud noise complaint from Linda's neighbors. They saw Ed leave. Later Ed would return and take Roger, Laurie, and Danny Bolstad to the Country Kitchen for breakfast. On the way from there home, Ed received a speeding ticket. In the morning, Jack Willis Nissalke woke up with June at Linda's and went to get something to eat. At mid-morning, they all heard the news. Ada had been murdered. Rumors were abounding that she had her head cut off. Jack and the others tried to get close to her house to see what was happening, but the block was already taped off. He drove Linda's car back to her house and was putting brakes on her car when policemen showed up to question all of them Jack, like the others, answered questions and showed his hands to them.

Over the next 20 years, Jack would grow up, raise a family, and continue to be interviewed by the Winona authorities about the murder of Ada Senenfelder. He always complied. Jack married Julie Prolo and helped her raise her 3 children. He made a living as a truck driver and pursued his love of racing. Jack stayed in Winona and developed lifelong friends, that would later support him after his conviction. One of of my trips to Winona, there was an endless stream of people willing to tell me stories of how good a friend Jack is. Mike Gierok, when he was small, had thrown a rock and broken a window at a used car lot. The owner threatened to go to the police. He asked Jack for the money to replace the money. Jack gladly gave it to him. Mike broke down and cried as he told me this. Does this mean Jack couldn't have killed Ada? No. But I will show you evidence he didn't. However, most killers leave a trail of violence and tell tale signs. For such a brutal murder, Jack never showed any signs he had a homicidal tendencies. On the other hand, upon meeting him, I found a kind, gentle, intelligent man, who was well liked. Count me as one of them.

Who was Ed Bolstad?

When Bobby Fort was taking his cushy deal in court on January 29, 1985, Edward John Bolstad was pleading "not guilty" to stabbing Richard Lynn on the exact same day. Lynn, 26, was a bouncer at the Country Connection. The newspaper accounts report that Ed was so drunk, he fell off his bar stool, got up and stabbed Lynn. When the police arrested Bolstad, 33 at the time, he cried out, "I hope I stabbed the fucker!" Later in the year, a few weeks after Ada was murdered, Ed would be found "not guilty". This unbelievable verdict came even after the bouncer identified Ed from the stand.

In the Bolstad family, Jimmy was the oldest, and kind of a leader. Ed came next whenever Jimmy was in jail or gone. The entire Bolstad family was mentored by their parents, Julius and Adeline. Even as youngsters, when they would get caught, Adeline would chide them as to how to shoplift or what ever the crime was, how to do it with out getting arrested. She was the 'Ma Barker' in Winona. Ed was the 'go to guy' for drugs in town. He was a frequent guest at Bobby Fort's house and made several deals with him and Earl Lemon.

As the parties got better at Jimmy's house, Ed was present at most of them, and soon attracted the attention of their neighbor, Rena Bambenek. When she caught Ed and Ada in bed together, she was very distraught, crying to Linda Parrish "Why does he do it?" After Ada had Jimmy arrested for allegedly having sex with her underage daughter, Ed knew something had to be done. Bobby Fort, before he was arrested, had told Ed and Earl Lemon, 'something needs to be done about Ada, she has to be shut up, she knows too much.'

The night Ada was murdered, Ed was at Linda's with several family members. The mood was light, although they found out Jimmy Bolstad was prison bound anyway. Through out the night people kept arriving until about 10:30 p.m., when Ed decided to leave the party. Several people heard his loud pipes on his Camaro go through the parking lot, including the police who came to ask they turn the juke box down. He would return about 1:30 am. At 12:45 am, Carol Przbylski, a waitress at the Happy Chef restaurant, noticed Ed come in the door. Carol had come to work at 11:00 p.m. said that Ed is his beige cords, and long sleeve checkered shirt was extremely dirty. He went straight to the pay phone and made a brief call. Then he received two calls on the house phone. Both calls were a female and the same one. Later Rena Bambenek would admit that she was the one who was calling him. She said that Ed wanted to know what the hell the cops were doing at Linda's. When he returned to the party, he seemed sober and lucent. He took his brother Roger, Laurie Nissalke, and his nephew, Danny, to the Country Kitchen for breakfast after 3:00 am. After breakfast, Ed was driving them home and got a speeding ticket.

The next day, Ed was noticeably different. He seemed nervous and excited. He cleaned out his dirty car, bought new clothes, threw a garbage bag of soiled clothes in a dumpster, and began to act morose. Family members began to worry he had killed Ada, and made numerous phone calls to that effect. The next several days were a nerve wracking experience for Ed Bolstad. The police impounded his car. He was brought in and video taped with multiple scratches on his hands and wrists. People came forward to admit that Ed had showered the night Ada was killed, Ed had tossed bloody clothes into a dumpster. He got drunk and pissed on Ada's grave, thinking he was about to go away to prison. He threatened the friends and family to keep shut or "you'll get the same as Ada got it."

Then a miracle happened. Weeks went by. Bobby Fort got out of jail. The police stopped coming by with search warrants. Months went by and 1985 came to an end with a cold Minnesota winter. No arrests were made in the death of Ada Senenfelder. Not even Ed Bolstad. For the next 20+ years, citizens would offer rumors and advice. The case stayed open as people in jail, some of them Bolstads, would try and bargain information about the murder to get a reduced sentence. The police followed every clue, every interview was carefully recorded, but no arrests were made. In the mean time, Bobby Fort died, as did Ed Bolstad.

2006

In 2006, the Winona County Attorney was Charles "Chuck" MacLean. Chuck had only one unsolved homicide on the books at the time, and it went back all the way to 1985. He went through the case again and saw absolutely no way to solve it after all this time. After he and his staff tried to breathe life into a very cold case, the only thing they could think of that would solve the case was one thing: money. Chuck went to the Bureau of Criminal Apprehension, a Minnesota state law division with greater resources and manpower. They, too, had been unable to solve this crime. He asked them to go to a citizens group, Spotlight On Crime, and request a reward prize, a very large prize. After the board met, the granted his request and gave the DA $50,000. If new evidence was forthcoming, maybe some new stories was what they needed. MacLean printed up wanted posters with Ada's picture on it and the following caption: Up to $50,000 reward is being offered leading to the arrest and conviction of person(s) responsible for the murder of Ada Frances Senenfelder. Ada Senenfelder, 40, mother of 5, was found stabbed to death in the bedroom of her Winona, Minnesota home on June 6, 1985. No evidence of robbery or sexual assault was present. However, the physical evidence from the case is being re-examined with today's modern forensic methods, and the results are breathing fresh life into this cold case. Law enforcement officials know that multiple witnesses have information that could assist in resolving this case. PLEASE HELP BRING CLOSURE TO THE FRIENDS AND FAMILY OF ADA SENENFELDER, AND BRING HER KILLER(S) TO JUSTICE. Anyone with information is asked to call the Winona Police Department at 507-454-4087, or the Minnesota Bureau of Criminal Apprehension Cold Case Unit at 651-793-7000 or 888-234-3692. www.spotlightoncrime.org.

Later, I would call the 651 number to ask Jeff Hanson what happened to the money. When I first started this investigative journey, this poster sounded impressive. In reality, the only new thing that Chuck had was the 50 grand. He had his team tack these posters up everywhere. There were ads on TV and he gave news conferences that sounded like "Law And Order", the TV show. Disappointingly, not many came forward. Chuck decided to take this to the people. He had investigators make a list of everyone the cops had ever talked to and go visit them. The list was long. Their marching orders were the same. Do the good cop-bad cop on everybody. They would come to their house, waving their badges, and chit chat a few short minutes and quickly bring up the reward money. They would sound like Publishers Clearing House. "We have this money, we just need a little help. We have this new DNA testing and almost have the case cracked." The people would always start off the same. "It was 20 years ago, I don't know anything. I didn't know anything then either." The investigators soon got frustrated and would intimidate them. The always wanted a DNA sample, "just to clear them." They went to the following list of people wondering who may have killed Ada:

Brently Johnson, Robert Smith, Donna Campbell, Lee Campbell, Vicki Wicka, Lynn Marie Nagel, Shelly Stoeckly, Randy Bolstad, James Bolstad, Brenda Howe, 'SP', June Bolstad, Roger Bolstad, Penny Bolstad, Tracy Larson, Laurie Nissalke, Rena Bambenek, Dennis Mickelson, Ozzie Mickelson, Bruce Howe, Ray Zeimer, Raymond Bolstad, Laurie Sayre, Daniel Bolstad, Mark Dooney, Carla Meier, Lenny Huwald, John Wise, Pam Cox, Brenda Nagel, Donald Hanson, Lynn Merrell, Darrell Kramer, Julie Peterson, Linda Hawley, Gary Casper, Gina Wood, Lori Kutchara, Linda Peterson, Karla Wilson, Ramona Abbott, Albert Bolstad, Kevin Bakewell, Richard Koenig, Viola Welch, Junior Benson, Jerome Gierok, Lavonne Thompson, Paula Stutzka, Gary Marks, Kenneth Warzecha, Lee Campbell, James Richmond, Steve

Googins, Jack Nissalke, Linda Parrish, Lori Phillips, Elizabeth Hokenstad, and Robert Neyers.

For a grand total of 59 humans and $50,000, they went to each one with their routine. Below is an excerpt from the interview with Brenda Howe, who was at the party of Linda Parrish when Ada was killed. Brenda was 15 at the time and looked younger. Still, the police didn't vary their approach.

On 9-27-06, by Jeff Mueller and Tom Williams:
TW- It's been on the news, we're reopening the investigation of the death of Ada Senenfelder.
BH- What do you want to know with me?
TW-Who did it?
BH- Oh! Tell me who did it?(laughs) I'd like to know, too.
TW- Well, it's really not up to us to say who did it. That's what we have to try and figure out and see if we have a theory as to who did it. It's just, ah, determining whether or not we can substantiate that from talking to people and physical evidence and that type of thing.
BH- Who did it? Danny Bolstad do it?
TW – Which Bolstad?
BH- Danny.
JM – We're kind of rehashing…
BH – I sat down myself and tried to figure this shit out. Ah, I would just went up there that night and ah, drank alcohol and got drunk. The next day got questioned by the cops. That's about as much as I know. And I'm sure you've read what I've said or what ever. A couple of different times. This would be when did I buy the house? 14 or 15 years ago a couple of detectives came down from ….St Paul or something.
JM- Can we sit down and actually talk?
BH- I'm like, what did I do down in Winona? I know I didn't do anything wrong.

Murder and Deceit

JM- No.

BH-I see this stuff come up on TV, ah you know, like the girl in LaCresent got her head cut off that kind a deal, there's bulletins left and ...

JM-There was bulletins you said, or was that..

BH-I don't know. We got like around town, new evidence, whatever, they're...

JM-give us some background on this...

BH-like blood in the back of Ed's car?

JM-Technology's come a long ways.

BH-Oh, I ain't gonna sit here all day and give you a spiel. I mean you guys probably know this Jim was in jail for ah, raping her daughter, some stuff like that.

JM-yes.

TW-He was in the LaCrosse jail at the time.

BH-so he wouldn't be the guy who did it?

JM-you wouldn't think so. But that group of people you were with, the Bolstad's?

BH-Yeah.

JM-You ever hear from them directly? The Nissalke's, the Bolstad's?

BH-No, I never heard from them.

JM-Okay, do you remember who all else was at the party that night?

BH-Danny, Ray, I don't know.

TW-Danny Bolstad, Ray Bolstad?

BH-Yeah, Ed and ...

TW-Ed Bolstad?

BH-Yeah and Jack and Linda...

TW-Jack Nissalke? Linda Nissalke? Linda Erickson?

BH-Um, I don't know if Dennis was there or not, I want to, I don't know what the story was, but Dennis and Laurie Bolstad went to

Ada's that night to pick up some ham for the next day, something like that.

JM- Who stayed all night, do you remember?

BH-Me and Bruce, and Ray, I don't know if Danny did, and Jack did.

JM-Jack Nissalke?

BH-Yeah, the cops last time said they found blood in the back seat of Edward's car.

JM-This is just stuff you're hearing?

BH-Edward, is he still alive or what?

JM-No, Edward's dead, he died.

BH-Oh he did?

JM-Brenda, if you're not telling us the truth, if you're holding something back, we're gonna make sure you're criminally charged.

BH-No, whoever did this, I don't understand things from the beginning, you know.

JM-And it would be worth 50 grand, you know.

BH-But I could not get to square one with Jimmy going to jail because of her testifying against him or what ever, you know what I mean?

JM-Sure.

TW-There's two venues here Brenda, $50,000 for any information that helps solve this thing, and there's the criminal aspect of this thing. Our county attorney said in the press conference, he said it's a race to the courthouse.

BH-Yeah.

TW-There's 10 people working on this right now.

JM-Just to fan out and talk to everyone that was involved. We can now eliminate people. What I want to ask you is if you would provide us a DNA sample? Just so we can do it for elimination purposes with you. So we can say "Hey, we know for sure you weren't even at the crime scene." Cause all it takes is me scraping the insides of you mouth to get a DNA sample and that's it.

BH-And what if these sick fuckers did something to me when I was passed out and out my shit there?

JM-I don't know, then we should…

BH-You know what I mean?

JM-We'd hash that over, you know what I mean?

BH-No you guys'll put anybody behind bars. I ain't got nothing to do with this shit.

JM-We don't necessarily think you did, what we could do…

BH-You know what I mean?

JM-is confirm that for us by the doing the DNA sample.

BH-I want to talk to the ones who were there while I was passed out, and if they're capable of something like this, know what I mean?

JM-No.

BH-I gotta think smart.

JM- I know what you mean as far as that goes. I wasn't there, so I don't know that you weren't there, and what this does is 100%. Then we don't have to worry about it. Otherwise we can't cross you off the list.

TW-We just fill out this form.

BH-I don't know.

JM-We swab this in your mouth and test it and then we know you weren't there, at the crime scene.

BH-And then what? You're never gonna talk to me again?

TW-Well I won't say that.

JM- We got that $50,000.

BH-This just ain't professional to me.

TW-Want us to do a blood draw?

BH-Jesus Christ I have bad luck.

JM-Ever watch TV shows?

BH-I don't…

JM-CSI?

BH-No, I don't…

TW-It's just a little swab.

BH-I don't…

JM-Like you said, Ada was…

BH-I watch TV on my…

JM-You heard Ada was stabbed, though…

BH-I heard her head was cut off.

JM-Her head wasn't cut off. The was a lot of blood and we can test that.

TW-If there's an unknown sample out there, then we can't eliminate yours.

BH-Come on you guys, I was 13 for Christ's sake.

JM- Tell you the truth a lot of this is just logistics.

BH-Come on you guys, do I get to keep something saying you did this, or something?

TW-We just document the fact you asked for it and seal it up right here in front of you.

BH-Nobody's had a problem with this?

JM-Well actually they have.

BH-You guys make me nervous. Some reason, who knows what could happen?

JM-Here's what it looks like Brenda, got your name on it and birthday.

BH-You want me to sign something?

JM-You don't need to sign something.

BH-Don't look very professional.

JM-It is what it is. I didn't make this up. I ain't gonna touch the part touching you. It goes right in your mouth.

(He scrapes her mouth)

TW-Brenda what we really wanted you to do was say was "this is who did it and this is how."

BH-Maybe I'll get really drunk Saturday night and it will come back to me.

Murder and Deceit

The entire interview took 54 pages and is one of the shorter ones. Most of the other 58 let the police take a DNA sample as well. None of them knew much about the case. All of this had the feel of traveling salesmen closing a deal on a product you didn't want. I have read the hundreds of pages of interviews and at the end of all this, they had nothing. The investigators were more aggressive with some, especially Linda Parrish, months later. They grew tired of the same answers and the dead ends. They needed a break, a big one. MacLean was spending a lot of Winona's money testing DNA. What were they testing it against? What was his plan? They went back several times and interviewed the same people and had no new tactic. Their basic plan was to *make* somebody talk. Oddly enough, many of these people had been interviewed about Ada at regular intervals for more than twenty years. No new leads had ever emerged.

2007

MacLean got lucky in 2007. When his aggressive team went to collect DNA from Jack Nissalke, they chose an early morning surprise. Jack had driven the night before to be in a car race that day. He was a truck driver and was exhausted when he got home in Winona. In bed with his wife, Jack was sound asleep when they came knocking hard. Julie got up and was felled by them in the narrow porch. Jack rose up and rushed out to see the commotion in his boxers. Seeing his wife lying there and trying to comprehend, he instinctively grabbed a pipe lying there. He dropped it as the police moved in to arrest him. Jack cursed them all as they led him away. They would file charges Jack for domestic terrorism, and would charge Julie with obstruction of justice. After an obscene amount of money spent, they would later both be found not guilty.

2008

A frustrated but victorious Chuck MacLean filed the first murder charges in the death of Ada Senenfelder and made the headlines on June 10, 2008. MacLean was a hero, about to close the books on a 23 year old cold case murder. This was newsworthy outside of the small town of Winona, and was a career maker. MacLean was a bright shinning star and would not let any crime go unpunished now. In a cell in the Winona Law Enforcement Center he had captured a vicious murderer, Jack Nissalke, at least that is what he told the newspaper and TV. MacLean began a campaign in the media to try Jack Nissalke. I only want to give you the headlines.

Murder Charges Filed in Senenfelder Slaying 6-10-08

Bail Set At $5 Million For Nissalke 6-11-08

Murder Charges Filed In 1985 'Cold Case' 6-11-08

Nissalke Bail Set At $5M In Cold Case 6-12-08

Nissalke Wants To See Evidence; County Attorney Says Grand Jury Must Indict Accused Killer First 6-24-08

Grand Jury Issues Indictments In Senenfelder Slaying; Three Face Charges in 23 Year Old Cold Case 7-02-08

Indictments Issued In 1985 Slaying 7-3-08

Nissalke Arraigned On 1st Degree Murder Indictment 7-7-08

Bail Remains Unchanged At 5 Million For Man Accused in 1985 Murder 7-08-08

Bail Set At 2 Million For '85 Suspect (Linda Parrish) 7-11-08

Woman Arraigned In Senenfelder Case 7-16-08

Jack Nissalke Hearing Postponed 8-1-08

Homicide Suspect Challenges Assault Case Evidence 8-20-08

Delays Push Back Nissalke Murder Case To February 9-04-08

Charges Refiled Against Nissalke's Wife 9-10-08

Accused Killer's Wife In Court 9-19-08

Julie Nissalke Arraigned 10-03-08

Nissalke In Court On Obstruction Charge 10-04-08

Judge Rejects Nissalke's Request To Dismiss 10-13-08

Nissalke Assault Charge Stands 10-14-08

Nissalke Pleads Not Guilty To Assault 11-6-08

Nissalke Pleads Not Guilty To Assault 11-7-08

Indictment Reading Is Hefty Challenge 12-9-08

A Tainted Jury Pool? Nissalke's Lawyer Seeks Change Of Venue 12-17-08

Nissalke Assault Trial Going Forward 12-14-08

Judge To Rule On Change Of Venue Request In Nissalke Case 1-6-09

Top Ten Stories Of 2008 12-31-08

Two Winona Men Charged With Murder 1-7-09

Nissalke Trial To Stay In Winona 1-7-09

No Jury Yet In Nissalke Assault Trial 1-13-09

Opening Statements Profane In Nissalke Trial 1-14-09

Attorney Charged With Cocaine Possession 1-14-09

Attorney Arrested At Courthouse Due To Cocaine 1-17-09

Lawyer In Coke Case Hires Attorney 1-30-09

Nissalke Sentencing Delayed 2-23-09

Nissalke Pleads Not Guilty 2-24-09

Nissalke Requests Denied 3-2-09

Trial Date Set: Nissalke To Face Jury May 18 3-3-09

Murder Suspect's Wife Pleads Not Guilty To Obstruction 3-3-09

Lawyer In Cocaine Case To Challenge Charges 3-6-09

Indictment Stands Against Accused Accomplice 3-17-09

Suspect In 85 Killing In Custody 3-17-09

Bolstad Extradited To Winona To Face Senenfelder Murder Charges 3-30-09

Bolstad Extradited To Face Murder Charges 3-31-09

Woman Pleads Not Guilty To Aiding Murder 4-1-09

Parrish Pleads Not Guilty 4-2-09

Nissalke Gets Probation For Terroristic Threats 4-2-09

Nissalke Gets Stayed Sentence, Probation 4-3-09

Lawyer Requests Venue Change For Murder Trial 4-27-09

New Venue Requested For Nissalke Murder Trial: More the 200 Witnesses Possible 4-28-09

Nissalke Trial Moved To Fillmore County 5-1-09

Ramsay, Winona Lawyer Challenges His Own Drug Arrest 5-5-09

Nissalke Trial Starts Today 5-28-09

The Average Joe doesn't even read the newspaper. He watches TV constantly. This happens to be a book, so I can't play the hundreds of times "NISSALKE, MURDERER" was flashed on the screen of every home with a TV in that part of the world. If this is all you know about Jack Willis Nissalke, how would you believe he could even possibly be innocent? Read the papers, Osama bin Laden—Terrorist, Jack Nissalke—Terrorist. MacLean had the odds finally going in his favor. All he needed was a motive, and some evidence.

I will tell you of the incredible story of the trial a little later, but first I want to tell you how hard it was for me to get any co-operation for this book.

A Wall Of Silence

When I first started to ask questions about why Jack was convicted, I had a laundry list of names that Jack's family compiled for me. I didn't know any of them and they didn't know me. I had absolutely no idea how to interview people or get them to talk about a murder trial. I was good at writing letters, so I tried that. I wrote dozens to the DA, and other people involved in the case. I mailed some every day, confident of getting lots of responses. I would cross more names off lists and search anywho.com for addresses. Naively, I was shocked when no one responded. I couldn't believe it. I called Jack's dad, Ron. He had a bunch of police papers he had scanned and started sending me those. On those I found more names. I contacted jurors. Not a single juror would talk. I marveled at this. If you had caught a cold blooded killer who was free for over 20 years and sent him away for life, wouldn't you be proud of that? What would be the motive to not break a silence? This was hard for several months. At the time of writing this, I have had lots of people talk to me, but the ones who don't have a reason I will share later in the book.

Meltdown

This story, and the love I encountered, triggered lots of emotions in me totally unexpected. For years I suffered from depression and have tried to deal with it in my own way. The idea of Jack, who was innocent, being in prison, never set right with me. In May of 2010, I started a blog, never thinking what it would become. The blog's story is incredible and I became devoted to telling Jack's story daily for months. This made me dig for more to have something to tell. My friends noticed that I was only talking and thinking about this more and more. After my trip to Minnesota in June, I returned with 20 years of crime notes and interviews. I also had lots of pictures. Crime photos and videos of Ada's dead body, with her lifeless eyes looking at me. I had pictures of the party and Ed Bolstad's car. I watched of video of Ed showing his scratched up hands to the police. I had become obsessed to the point of knowing about this case was all that was on my mind. The dreams and nightmares began. When I began to know that Jack was innocent, I had a plan for the structure of the book. I only wanted to show you the evidence that proved Jack couldn't have done this. Something inside me was trying to tell me something else. Ada began to talk to me in my dreams. She would ask me to solve the murder, bring the real killers to the light of day. I knew this was impossible, as so many were dead I believe were involved. She still would appeal to me. How could I do this? The pressure got to me after a few months. I began to feel personally responsible if Jack didn't get his freedom. After too much drinking and out-of-control depression, I took a ten day break. I examined my motives for doing this. It wasn't money, I wasn't making any. It was love.

Murder and Deceit

The Trial of Jack Nissalke

The *Winona Daily News* declared on April 28,2008, the trial to punish the murderer of Ada Senenfelder was ready to begin— after a 23 year delay. The newspaper promised a spectacle that would include 200 witnesses, hundreds of exhibits, DNA evidence, and plenty of fireworks in the courtroom. Chuck Ramsay, Jack's attorney, pleaded for a change of venue. He made the point that everyone in Winona had been told that Jack had probably killed Ada. On May 1, the trial was moved to Fillmore County. The quaint town of Preston would get to decide the fate of Jack Nissalke. Judge Robert Benson agreed that the heavy press coverage, the endless press conferences given by the DA, and the prejudiced statements the law enforcement officers had given to the citizens of Winona for the past year. As far as Winona County was concerned, Jack was guilty, and there was no need for a trial. Jack had been in jail for a year now, and had not killed Ada Senenfelder.

Linda Parrish and James Bolstad had also been charged with aiding and abetting Jack in Ada's murder. They would be offered a deal to win their freedom. Jack insisted he was innocent and would not entertain a deal. On May 18, the trial opened with 49 motions. One of the first ones to be addressed was how Jack was brought to the courthouse. MacLean and Gort had Jack transported from Winona to Preston in a convoy of Sheriff cars, chained and shackled for all to see. Ramsay argued this would prejudice anyone who saw him brought to the courthouse this way. The only other time people would see a man this way was as Hannibal Lector in "Silence Of The Lambs". Judge Benson would deny the motion as he would every other motion the defense asked for. The other motion Ramsay filed was to exclude the new ground breaking DNA tests the posters had proclaimed. Tom Gort had the dubious of job of introducing Y-STR DNA to a jury. There are five types of testing, Y-STR is usually helpful in sexual assault cases where there are multiple attackers. It excludes female DNA and is used on the mixture. Chuck Ramsay argued that people watched TV so much they would not understand how this worked and would confuse them. He was right and the judge once again said no way, the Y-STR was in.

Jury selection began and the slow process tried to find the rare person who did not already believe that Jack was guilty. By May 22, 12 jurors were seated and three alternates were ready. Opening statements were delayed as the judge was deciding about the DNA testing. The Y-STR can not identify a single contributor and definitely not a female. Now, what had they tested? Were they testing another man's blood found on Ada's body, or clothes, or bed, or walls? Was it something from the bloody hand print on the front door or the light switch. Was it semen or saliva? Was it a hair left by the killer? No, all that was now gone, lost by the police. What these scientists were analyzing was the only thing left, an ash tray full of cigarette butts. Cigarette butts? Yes. Now, Jack admitted to being there when Jim Bolstad's Probation Officer was at Ada's house on June 5, 1985. He did smoke a cigarette while he was there. The BCA ID'd several matches positively to the ashtray. There are 17 points to match. Jack matches 4. That's it. They are arguing whether or not to allow the jury to hear that Jack's can not be excluded from the DNA test, when in reality it says that there is a 25% chance Jack smoked in Ada's house sometime. There, that's it. This is the ground breaking new technology promised on the poster. I even called Amy Liberty, from the BCA, who testified at Jack's trial, and asked her to talk to me. She's another one who doesn't want to talk, at least to me. Try to imagine a killer with a knife, covered in blood, smoking to relax, before leaving the crime scene. The judge ruled the Y-STR was in.

In opening arguments, Tom Gort told the jury that Jack left the party at Linda's house and killed Ada. This is in spite of pictures and testimony proving this is a lie. This is the reason I titled this book, *Murder and Deceit*. Gort and MacLean know this is not true. They know Jack did not leave the party. They know Jack had no motive. Deceit is the twisting of facts or words. Deceit is a nice way to say liar. I contend that Jack was framed for this. Chuck Ramsay told the jury of at least 4 other people with a real motive to kill Ada, and that Jack had talked to the police willingly about this for over 20 years. Jack had nothing to hide. Gort would shout that Ada was killed by Jack because Jim Bolstad was in jail. Gort would say that Bolstad had ordered the hit, as he was in charge of a supposed crime family. He claimed that Jack was sweaty and had cut his hand. Gort outlined a conspiracy so organized that the masterminds even had the forethought to have a party to "get their stories straight." Chuck Ramsay recounted how Jack had been interviewed dozens of times over the 20 year span. What changed in 2006 to put him in jail for this crime, he asked? $50,000. He urged the jury to consider the truthfulness of any witnesses who suddenly came forward to testify after 20 years of silence.

The first to try and win the money was Shelly Stoeckly. She was Jack's girlfriend up until the week before Ada's killing. She walked into the courtroom, swore on the Bible, and said she knew Jack killed Ada for over 20 years. Before she could get any closer to the money, MacLean stopped the trial, had the jury removed, and red faced told the judge that Craig Holm, the investigator for Jack's legal defense had 'intimidated' one of their "star" witnesses, Rena Bambenek. Chuck was afraid Rena would be so damaged by his tactics that his case against Jack would suffer. I talked to Craig about this and read his report. Here is what really happened. Craig found Rena in a secret motel location MacLean had hidden her away from Winona. When Craig found her, she was drunk from the whiskey in her 7-11 Big Gulp cup. He tried to talk to her and didn't get very far. Rena was slurring her words and defensive. She didn't say much and he left. What was Chuck so outraged about? He had been rehearsing Rena down there and paying for her expenses so she could 'get her story straight'. For hours they coached her to say "I saw Jack that night, sweaty, bloody, with a knife." Rena would lapse as she admitted she had not seen him at all that night. The would badger her "we need you say this." MacLean knew she was fragile with the made up story and was terrified she had been found out. He got the judge to spank Craig Holm and warned him to 'back off'. This was Chuck's day in the sun and Rena was his secret weapon; plus he had spent a lot of taxpayer money on motel rooms and whiskey. He had a lot invested in her 'story'. Back to Shelly: she went to say that she was very intoxicated at the times she was testifying about, and had a grudge against Jack. She stuck by her story. She had known Jack was a murderer for the whole time. She also admitted to going with Jack to get Ada to recant and hope Jimmy got out of jail. When Ramsay asked her if she was part of a conspiracy to get a witness to tamper with her testimony, the judge admonished her to consult an attorney herself before incriminating herself. At that point, she burst into tears and Chuck MacLean cried "Witness intimidation!"

When Jack broke up with Shelly Stoekly, he dated June Bolstad, Jimmy's sister. She was the next witness to say she always knew Jack was the killer of Ada Senenfelder. It seemed now everyone in Winona "always knew he did it." When Ramsay questioned her, he asked why she failed to mention this in the volumes of testimony she gave police in 1985, 1992, 2006, and 2008? He even played a tape where she admitted she didn't know who killed Ada. MacLean tried to bolster her up and got her to say they never asked her directly if she knew who killed Ada. She also had to change her statement that Linda Parrish paid Jack $50,000 to kill Ada to $5,000. Pam Cox got up next, and told how she helped Linda Parrish clean her apartment. She said at the same time Jack asked her to help look for his knife. She apologized for not saying anything because she is afraid of Jack.

Dr. William McNeil testified next. He claimed there were multiple attackers. He pointed out her glasses were on the night stand, and the different angles of the wounds. The depth varied and so did the blood splatter. He admitted that the knife from her kitchen, found lying on her chest, may have delivered the fatal blow. Interestingly enough, this same Doctor, 6-8-85, told Al Meuller, that he thought one knife could have delivered all the blows. Now he testifies that there were multiple attackers. Did they pass the knife around like a joint? This is hard to imagine. The evidence does point to multiple attackers, in spite of the scenario with one knife Bill suggests.

On June 14, Rena Bambenek walked to the stand and took her oath to tell the truth. She testified that she saw Jack the night Ada was murdered, in her parking lot, with a cut hand, seeking a knife he had lost. Rena said his hand was wrapped in a towel with bloody stains. She claims that Jack said "she died slow." Gort and MacLean were almost home here. They got her to hold together and tell it just like they wanted. This would have been very good had not the legal system allows for cross examination. Jack's attorney asked Rena if the morning she found out Ada was dead, did she drive Jack and Linda over to the crime scene and try to find out what was going on? Rena said yes. When Ramsay asked why she didn't run up to the cops and tell them to arrest Jack after he had confessed to her the night before, Rena was stumped. Rena admitted that the DA had helped her "recover" her lost memory and left it at that. Ramsay also asked why she never mentioned Jack in years of interviews that followed? She said she was scared of him then, but not anymore since he was locked up. She also confessed she did not attend the party where Jack was and never left her apartment that night. Ramsay also asked her why she had changed her story so much over the years. Rena just shrugged and seemed confused. Ramsay almost triggered a mistrial as he played a tape where Rena mentions she had taken a lie detector test (she failed). The judge reprimanded Ramsay and the trial kept going.

The jury listened to several hours of tape that gave her newest version, in case she forgot.

On June 21, Dennis Fier took the stand. Now retired, Fier spent his career with the BCA, and a good part of it investigating the murder of Ada Senenfelder. Most of the interviews I read from day one forward had his name on them. There are hundreds of pages Fier authored trying to build a case to solve the only unsolved murder in the county. What was his conclusion? He always thought the strongest motive to have her silenced was from her having Bobby Fort jailed. Fier admitted they turned the group Jack was part of upside down, with search warrants and interviews, and came up empty. MacLean and Gort never wanted to talk about any other theory but Jack. They intentionally ignored the findings of the BCA, FBI, and ATF. All of them agreed that Bobby Fort had something to do with Ada's killing. The Winona DA only wanted to pursue the most unlikely of all theories.

On June 23, Anne Ciecko, a forensic scientist took the stand. Chuck Ramsay tried to get the Y-STR findings from the court room, and the judge should have never allowed this, but once again, carte blanche was given to the prosecutors. The original investigators harvested lots of DNA evidence from the scene. Where most of that is now, has never been answered. Most of it would exonerate Jack now and identify the killer. Anne described the ashtray and how Jack's DNA matches some of the DNA points in the mix there. Jack admits to being there with Shelly, June, and Linda. and smoking while Ada talked to the probation officer. Under oath, she said,"other than the cigarette butts, I have no match to Jack's DNA to the evidence found there". Amy Liberty, from the BCA, also said testified that Y-STR can not identify a single donor, and excludes women. I called Amy several times to discuss this at length for the book, and she never returned my calls. Again, I wonder why? Amy admitted Jack was among 10 men linked to the butts. Ramsay asked her what percentage of men in general might be excluded from this test, maybe as much as 50%? She said yes. As much as 10%? She didn't know. Liberty also said some of the DNA collected may have come from BCA agents working the crime scene.

On June 29, the prosecutors played the tapes they recorded between Jack and his wife. I have listened to many hours of these and always ended up crying. First of all, I felt I was violating the private conversations between a man and his wife as they went through the hardest days, weeks, and months imaginable. Most times Jack is listening to bad news from the home front, and no way to deal with any of it. You can hear his voice as his spirits sink lower and lower. Most of the conversation are about nothing to do with the charge of murder. On some of Jack's lowest days as he knew they were listening in, he would say that he should tell all, bring down the others. This would be played for the jurors and labeled his "confession."

On June 28, the *Winona Daily News* ran an article titled "The Nissalke Effect: Murder trial costly for for Winona Police, courts." It is one of this newspaper's only critical article featuring MacLean and Gort. It details how MacLean had gutted the courthouse to conduct this madness, and left the real crimes on hold. It laments how out of the three judges it takes to run the court at a bare minimum, there are two. The entire legal system was put on hold until at least August, and would resume way behind. The article ponders the problems this causes, including the six DA's normally running that office is now at three. MacLean is now at a crossroads that he has to win, at any cost. If he returns to Winona with anything other than "guilty", they will burn him alive.

On June 29, Steve Pagel took the stand. He contradicted Rena Bambenek's story that she saw Jack the night of the murder with his hand wrapped in a towel, bleeding. She claimed that he asked Steve to help look for his lost flashlight. Steve, under oath, said Jack 'never in his life' asked to look for a flashlight, and insisted he did not see him that night. He did however, remember Ed Bolstad coming to his apartment while he was having sex with his girlfriend, and asking them to wash his 'wet' clothes. Steve said he never went out that night. Tom Gort questioned his memory, but Pagel said he was clear on that.

On July 1, 2009, the defense rested. Jack did not take the stand, as his attorney thought he had the case clearly won. The closing arguments were high drama as Tom Gort painted Jack as a sadistic murderer for hire, who tortured Ada at length before stabbing her to death. He also claimed the killing was premeditated even though one of Ada's own knives was used to stab her. The jury now had 7 weeks of testimony, 10,000 pages of witness statements and 'evidence'. The were going to be sequestered over the 4th holiday weekend if a quick verdict was not reached. They got the case at 5 p.m. and came back four hours later, including an hour and a half for pizza and a smoke break. At 9:00 p.m. they came back in the courtroom with a guilty verdict. Jack was taken away. His family walked up the courthouse steps a short time later only to have Chuck Ramsay deliver the bad news. They went home and donated the food they had bought for a homecoming cook out to a homeless shelter. Jack Willis Nissalke went to prison on a life sentence.

Sarah Elmquist

There are two newspapers in Winona, *Winona Daily News*, and the *Winona Post*. While the *Daily News* did a fair job of covering Jack's trial, they did a huge amount of damage to his credibility before the trial. However, the *Post* has a writer named Sarah Elmquist who covers the crime beat in Winona. She won Investigative Reporter of the Year for Minnesota in 2007. Her articles about the murder trial was very different from her seat in the court room. During the trial Sarah filed the following report.

NISSALKE MAY WIN by Sarah Elmquist

Defense attorneys for Jack Nissalke hammered away at witnesses this week, questioning their credibility and memory of events that happened in 1985, when Nissalke is accused of fatally stabbing Ada Frances Senenfelder. Prosecutors argue that Nissalke left a party, where he was drinking, to silence the snitch who had sent his friend and coconspirator James Bolstad to jail after the woman reported he'd molested her daughter. But in the nearly 25 years since Senenfelder's death, many of the state witnesses have changed their stories about what happened that night – a fact that played a large role in Nissalke's defense thus far. Some of the state's key witness testimony seemed anticlimactic Thursday, when statements Nissalke is accused of making about the murder were less dramatic than what prosecutors said jurors would hear during opening statements. Rena Bambenek's testimony that she saw Nissalke the morning after the murder with a bloody cloth wrapped around his hand, looking for a knife he had lost was challenged. Defense attorney, Chuck Ramsay showed statements she had made to police prior to 2006 in which she never mentioned seeing him and repeatedly said she knew nothing about the crime, and that she wasn't afraid of Nissalke. The defense alleges that Bambenek didn't offer information until the $50,000 reward was offered for information which could lead to a conviction in the case, and that even then she changed her story—-first telling police Nissalke's hand was bleeding when he punched a wall. Also in 2006 she told police that Nissalke went to Senenfelder's house to get money from under the floor boards and when he didn't find any, he killed her. Ramsay asked Bambenek if that memory was a mistake, which she admitted. When asked if she had other such 'false memories', after nearly a quarter century, Bambenek said, "Oh definitely." Bambenek also admitted that the police pressured her by telling her she might be a suspect when she couldn't offer information about the case in the years after the crime, adding that after that she told them she'd seen Nissalke with the bloody rag. "They haven't implied I was a suspect since." In fact, Bambenek admitted the police told her she'd be their "superstar" in the case. Another piece of testimony prosecutors presented to jurors was about things Nissalke allegedly said a week or two after the murder while drinking at Prairie Island campground drinking with friends. Donna (Bolstad) Campbell, sister to accused coconspirator James Bolstad, took the stand Thursday. She said she didn't remember what brought it on, but that Nissalke said "I'll get you like I got Ada." But Campbell said she couldn't remember any other details about the alleged conversation, and defense attorneys allowed her to refresh her memory by reviewing transcripts of previous interviews, a common practice in this trial. After reading through previous statements Campbell looked up. "Maybe that's why I was so scared." Campbell said that what she'd told police was this: "I'll get you like I did Ada, once through the heart, something to that effect." During opening statements, prosecutors first words were "Three times in the neck, once in the heart", allegedly quoting Nissalke's words that day at Prairie Island. But witness testimony proved to be less dramatic, and another witness who was there at the time told a bit of a different story. Another witness, Linda Petersen, testified last week that she was at the party at Prairie Island, and she remembered more of the conversation which allegedly occurred over a picnic table. She said Nissalke told her at the time she was 'put out', to which she laughed and quipped back. Then she said Nissalke took out a knife, and put it in the picnic table. And although she couldn't remember his exact words, he said that she could get stabbed or cut up like Ada, not as prosecutors said in the opening statements, "like I cut Ada." Petersen refreshed her memory after that testimony, but what she found in her old testimony was exactly the testimony she just given. In a trial where most of the state's witnesses have had to review prior statements many times, Petersen presented what might seem the clearest memory of events in the case. Ramsay also attempted to dismiss the alleged statements Nissalke made as off colored jokes. He also asked Campbell whether their were rumors and cruel jokes going round at the time. A visibly shaken Campbell said "Yes, there were a lot of rumors that were very hurtful at the time," she said, and then burst into tears. Bruce Howe, who attended the party at accused coconspirator Linda (Erickson) Parrish's apartment the night of the murder, also testified Thursday. He said he didn't remember much about that night and didn't know anything about the murder, but said he didn't remember anyone leaving or coming back from the party, including Nissalke. Prosecutors allege that Nissalke, along with James Bolstad and Parrish, left the party that night and stabbed Senenfelder to death. After tape recording a meeting with a Probation Agent earlier in the day in which Senenfelder recanted her accusations against Bolstad, prosecutors say that Nissalke and Parrish learned it hadn't worked. Bolstad would remain in jail and his Probation Agent would still pursue the alleged molestation as a Probation violation. It was after learning this, prosecutors allege Nissalke killed Senenfelder. Defense attorneys have suggested a different story, one that points to Ed Bolstad, the now deceased brother of James Bolstad, and others as possible perpetrators. One witness testified that Ed Bolstad admitted he blacked out on the night on the murder, woke up in the morning in his car parked by Parrish's apartment, and needed someone to wash his clothes the next day. Testimony has also shown that Ed Bolstad and Senenfelder were lovers at the time of her death. Keep reading as the trial unfolds.

Deceit

The title of this book is *Murder and Deceit*, and I have shown you the interview of Brenda Howe in 2006 and now want to show you more than an example but how MacLean went after people in their homes with scare tactics and underhandedness. It is not pretty. The first example involves Linda Parrish, the host of the so-called party the night Ada died. The reason I refer to it as so-called is this was not an organized event but a nightly occurrence that happen at her apartment, the Bolstad place, and sometimes even Ada's house on 4th Street. Prairie Island was also a favorite of this ever changing group.

When I first started this journey to find out what happened, Linda was one of the people I wanted to talk to. After numerous phone calls and emails, she told me anything I asked of her and was willing to meet. In September, 2010, on my second trip to Minnesota, she talked to me at a coffee shop where I had set up residence. Linda gave me the afternoon as she talked about her life. She was born across the Mississippi River in Prairie Du Chien, Wisconsin. Her family moved to Winona when she was in the second grade. She grew up here and married Wayne Erickson when she was just 18. Early in their marriage, Wayne fell through the ice and died one winter. Linda, now a young widow, started life over again through this tragedy, little knowing what lie ahead. In March of 1985, she moved into an apartment in Winona, and began to socialize. To celebrate their birthday, her twin sister took her to the Country Connection and April 24th. That night she met the Bolstad family who found out she was lonely and had Wayne's insurance money.

The days after Ada's murder, Linda co-operated with the investigation. She had been a friend to Ada in the few weeks she had known her, and wanted to help any way she could. Linda even drove her truck to the Law Enforcement Center and let them examine it. She gave endless statements, and was eager to answer questions, just as Jack Nissalke did. The police never solved the case and Linda went on with her life. After Jack was wrongly convicted, Chuck MacLean would post a letter on the DA's website, crowing that this was the result of decades of police work. Nothing could be further from the truth. I have read the interviews all these people kept giving and there was nothing new, with the exception that all the evidence pointed right at Bobby Fort, and Rena Bambenek kept changing her story.

In 2006, Linda was living in Florida when she got news her mother had cancer. She moved back to Prairie Du Chien and right into the mouth of a monster. Soon after arriving, at a family get together, Jay Rassmussen and Sue Linkmeyer showed up unannounced. They caused quite a commotion banging on the door, yelling loudly, and flashing their badges. Linda asked them what they wanted, and upon learning they had question about a 20 year old murder, she asked the repeatedly to leave and set another time. Angrily, they left and met her at a gas station the next day. They drove Linda around and began to hurl insults and accusations at her, hoping she might confess to something. "We know you killed Ada, we have you in her house that night, we have your fingerprints and DNA all over the place!" Linda called their bluff and asked to see any of this fiction. She finally asked to be arrested or let go. Sue Linkmeyer became red-faced and started screaming at her. When you read most of the other interviews, they were in control and retaliated when someone challenged them. Linda tried to reason with them and asked if this was true, why didn't they arrest her now? Dejected and angry, they let her go, after accusing her of 1st degree murder and never advising her of her rights or the need of legal help. MacLean was incensed as well. Within a week, he had her arrested for 1st degree murder and set her bail at $5 million dollars, the same as Jack's. With no evidence against her, MacLean had her sit in jail 14 months. A group on Minnesota lawyers studied her case as a project. Their conclusion?

Linda was innocent. However, Linda was part a crucial plan to frame Jack. Her court appointed lawyer brought her the only deal: life in prison or testify against Jack. The reward? get out now! She took the deal without the DA having to prove anything. Linda only wanted to breathe air on the streets again. She felt she would die in prison and bent to their corrupt will.

Linda Parrish had nothing to do with the death of Ada Senenfelder. Nothing. Now, thanks to Chuck MacLean, she bears the mark of a convicted murderer. Several times she broke down and cried, and we had to stop. She is riddled with guilt over taking the deal to railroad Jack. Linda will live with the pain the DA inflicted on her to just 'close the case'. It broke my heart to witness the grief another innocent person encountered by the harshness of this county's legal system.

James Bolstad

In the master plan to try Jack Nissalke for murder, MacLean and Gort needed to make a jury believe that Ada Senenfelder's brutal murder was a revenge ordered hit commanded by the gang leader- James Bolstad. In the fall of 2006, Jay Rassmussen and Denny Fier took Sarah Berg as a stenographer across the Mississippi bridge to LaCrosse, Wisconsin. Jimmy was on Probation and they met with him and his Probation Officer, and had the following interview. This is the first one, and while I'm giving you excerpts, they are in context. The reason being is this interview is 145 pages and quite long. My blog, www.suicidecowboy.wordpress.com has the complete 145 pages, so if you have the time, read the entire body. To recap who Jim is, he is the oldest of Julius and Adeline Bolstad. Jim was in jail at the time Ada was murdered, since Ada had told police he was having sex with her underage daughter. Bolstad was on probation, and on the day before the killing, Ada signed a letter recanting this in front of the probation agent, and several friends. The letter was of no value as the agent still revoked Jim, and sent him away. The theory MacLean and Gort told the jury was Linda hired Jack to kill Ada for revenge because she and Jim were a couple at the moment.

This interview takes place on 9-27-06, at Jim's home. JB is James Bolstad, JR is Jay Rassmussen, and DF is Denny Fier.

JB- I don't know why you want to talk to me, I was in jail at the time. I've got a hell of an alibi.
JR- Yeah.
DF- How are you doing, Jim?
JB- I just had 7 bypasses, and they just took off my left leg. They just took and I had new arteries put in. They, you know cut my leg from my ankle all the way up to my stomach, and cut the bottom of my heart off and put all new, the main artery down through.

DF- Oh.

JB- And then when they kept me on heavy blood thinners, and they didn't tell me about it, and they cut the main artery out of my right leg, and I bled to death and died.

DF- Oh.

JR- Well in that case, it's good to see you.

JB- (laughs) Yeah.

DF- You seem to be doing good. You're ah, sober.

JB- Well, you wouldn't believe it, I've been through every treatment program-

JR- Well, you know why we're here today.

JB- Yeah, I couldn't believe it, I seen it on the news last night.

JR- Yeah.

JB- She was an OK woman. I didn't know if you guys knew it but her sister and her ma run whore house across the river. That Bluff siding tavern?

JR- Who ran that?

JB- Her ma and her sister. It was a whore house across the river.

JR- Well, anyways we're just looking over this case, we're looking into everything. You saw the news, the new technology..

JB- Yeah, I seen it on TV.

JR- ...with DNA and stuff. We think we got a great shot at solving this thing.

JB- You do?

JR- Yeah.

JB- Good.

JR- And what we're doing is, obviously everybody's all ready talked to the police back in '85. And we're talking again, al lot of stuff's happened, we think people are more apt, to give us help on the case.

JB- Right.

JR- We're expecting back from the DNA of crimes, like testing it back at the state..

JB- Right.

JR- we can get good statements from people, and maybe people remember stuff, or there're more apt to talk now.

JB- Right.

JR- Do you think that's a good idea?

JB- I think it's a damn good idea.

JR- And then there's that $50,000.

JB- I'd like to have that (laughs). She was a good friend of my ma. So was her husband before the thing with her kids. She used to come over to my house and clean and stuff all the time.

JR- and it looked like she cleaned a lot of people's houses.

JB- That's what she did, house clean you know, she never charged me nothing. And she's come over with buckets of chicken, and yeah, you know who's money it was though? Bobby Fort. I think I'd already told you that.

JR- Let's go chronological here. Start, is June 5, 1985, that's a big day in history, what can you tell me..

JB- Is that when it happened? I don't even remember when it happened, to tell you..

JR- June 5, recall a little bit, June 5 was the night Linda Erickson had a party at her house.

JB- That's, I was in jail.

JR- Yeah, you guys apparently called each other, and she had told you she's..

JB- She didn't tell me about no parties.

JR- Oh, she didn't tell you about any parties?

JB- Not no party, nuh-uh.

JR- What did she say?

JB- She just called and talked and stuff, you know, she didn't call and talk that much, and then she started going with that, uh, Nissalke.

JR- So you got locked up around the end, middle May 20, or 21?

JB- I don't remember even. She wouldn't come see me about 3 times, she helped me get a lawyer and then he wanted more money, and she said "that's it, I'm done with you." We never seen each other since.

JR- Was that, the murder happened on the night of June 5, or early June 6. Was she going out with Jack at that time?

JB- I heard he was going over there as soon as I was locked up.

JR- Okay.

JB- See the reason I get locked up, somebody called in and said I was drinking down to Winona. And I'm pretty sure it was Jack who turned me in. Cause he wanted Linda. Linda had a lot of money.

JR- And Jack wanted it.

JB- Jack wanted it. I know he tapped in, cause he was going with her when I got revoked.

JR- Even so, did you and Linda talk on the phone quite a bit?

JB- No, not a whole lot. I think maybe she called me 15 times maybe.

JR- Did you ever call out to her?

JB- Yeah I called, but I had to call through Rena to get through to her.

JR- When ever you wanted to call Linda, you went through Rena?

JB- Rena was side by side, she lived next to me.

JR- Rena was your next door neighbor?

JB- Right, I had to call her cause they didn't pay no phone bills.

JR- So, Jim, do you recall that night at all? Talking to Linda?

JB- Not no June 5th I don't.

JR- How'd you find out about Ada's murder?

JB- Rena told me.

JR- You found out about the murder from Rena?

JB- Yeah.

JR- Had you been talking to Linda after the murder?

JB- We were already broke up.

JR- You and Linda?

JB- Yep.

JR- Well you and Jack were pretty good friends, right?

JB- No, we weren't good friends. They, ah used hang around my brother and stuff.

JR- Who, which brother?

JB- Edward.

JR- So Jack and Edward were more friends than you and Jack?

JB- Yeah.

JR- What did Ada have to do with getting you in jail? I read some allegations and stuff.

JB- That she had her kids over at my place, her daughter stayed there two days or something.

JR- Helen.

JB- You got me.

JR- But it was Ada's daughter?

JB- Yeah. Ada slept on the couch, no big deal, she was lonely.

JR- You ever talk to anybody about this murder?

JB- I don't even go to Winona. I haven't talked to Jack or Linda in 21 years.

JR- I find that hard to believe. Denny worked this case back then, but I'm a new person, and I read you're the head of a family and all these people and you say you haven't even talked to them?

JB- I didn't say I haven't talked to no one in 21 years, I don't know where you're getting this from.

JR- You haven't talked about this murder?

JB- Why would we talk about it?

JR- What do you think, then?

JB- Well, you know I got two suspicions, and if it's worth, I don't think we're going to get the 50,000, but maybe I will, I can remember his name, him and Bobby Fort, Bobby Fort used him a lot, he was 22, 23, he always said he was going to kill her.

JR- And this would be who again?

JB- He used to, when Ada would go to the toilet, he used to screw her. You know, right in Bobby Fort's house. I never seen it, but that's what I heard. He'd actually make her bend over and he'd screw her and everything. I heard it from his own mouth, "I'm going to kill that fucking bitch." She was taking Bobby Fort's money, so I figure he's going to get Bobby Fort's money or what.

JR- He had a lot of money?

JB- Everybody thought he did.

JR- Do you know what he did for a living?

JB- Bobby Fort?

JR- Yeah.

JB- Stole antiques and stuff, stolen hides.

JR- He went to prison for that?

JB- Yeah, um uh, I don't remember the guy's name but his son just died too. They were buying hot hides all the time, that's why I thought Bobby Fort was worth a fortune. But I heard he burned his house down, or I heard his son burned it down for him.

JR- You had second suspicion, right?

JB- Yeah I always thought Linda paid Jack to do it.

JR- So then what? Jack kills Ada and what happens next?

JB- See that's what I don't..

JR- What would they get from that?

JB- Well I had a sneaky suspicion, you know Bobby Fort had this kid you know, he's hired a lot of people to do stuff.

JR- Well Bobby Fort and Ada were pretty much history at this time. I mean he was pretty much out of her life.

JB- Oh no, she, Bobby Fort, Ada was taking care of Bobby's money.

JR- Right up till she died?

JB- His checks and everything came to her.

DF- Bobby Fort was in jail when Ada died.

JB- I know, but this, they, his checks, she was getting his checks.

JR- Okay.

JB- And she was spending the money on us. And Bobby Fort found out about it. He said "I'm going to get.." He was going to get me.

JR- So Ada was spending her money, she would spend money on you guys?

JB- She was spending Bobby Fort's porch money.

JR- On like parties and stuff?

JB- Right, she used to buy chickens and half barrels of beer. She just wanted friends you know, she was a good woman, just a little funny, you know.

JR- So you don't think Ed or Roger or any of your friends?

JB- Oh, no, no. Roger never hung around with us.

JR- Any way Ed could have done it?

JB- No, Ed wouldn't hurt a fly. Everybody loved Ed. He did love his drinking though.

JR- What would you think Jim, if we run these tests and it's Ed's blood right next to Ada's body?

JB- That I couldn't believe, she was, she, Eddie was her friend.

JR- I'm just saying, proposing that, you know.

JB- I just couldn't believe it.

JR- Cause it's a possibility. Our County Attorney's going to take a look at everybody's statements, and we wouldn't want anybody to lie to us, because there'd be charges for that.

JB- That would stun me, cause I always had the suspicion Linda paid Jack to do it.

JR- Did you know that they had a search warrant on Ed?

JB- No, I never knew that.

JR- Denny, you want to say something?

DF- We're going to back here a ways. There's probably an easier way for you to get that 50,000.

JB- Okay.

DF- I'm going to refresh your memory a little bit, okay?

JB- Okay.

DF- You did call Linda the night of the 5th. This is the night..

JB- The 5th?

DF- You called her and they having a party and you were pissed off about it, which you had every right to be.

JB- Mmmm hmmm.

DF- "What the hell are you guys doing", those were your words.

JB- It was my house, they wrecked it.

DF- It wasn't your house, it was Linda's house.

JB- Oh, may be it was Linda's house. Yeah, right.

DF- Yeah, yeah, everybody was there. It was Danny, Raymond, Ed and Roger and..

JB- Roger didn't hang around with us then.

DF- Yeah, he was there. He got pretty stiff that night. Jack was there and Linda was there.

JB- When I went to, when I, I got locked up.

DF- Now I tell you, do you remember that phone call?

JB- You know really to tell you the truth. I don't quite place it. I don't remember, I'm kind of remembering, I think I, but I don't remember calling her house.

DF- Well you did.

JB- Okay.

DF- There was quite a lengthy phone call that evening. You told Linda, "It doesn't matter if you get to Ada to change that letter". You remember that?

JB- Yeah cause it was …

DF- "it doesn't matter cause I'm going to prison anyway."

JB- Yeah.

DF- You remember that part?

JB- Yep, I remember that part now.

DF- Now we're coming back.

JB- Yep, now it's coming.

DF- I'll, let's be more specific about this paying Jack.

JB- I, I uh can't, I can't prove that.

DF- Well, how are we going to prove it?

JB- Ah, well that's just it, I mean he got her, I mean why would you, you know, cause we're talking marriage and everything all the time. And then you know, and then, when I, you're right, you're right. I was madder than hell that Jack was there. Cause he, I, I knew he was after her. And I thought she'd kicked him out. You know? But she told me she'd kicked him out.

DF- Who? Jack?

JB- Yeah.

DF- Well I'm sure he was sniffing round her.

JB-Right.

DF- We're talking about the night Ada died.

JB- Okay.

DF- Because this is very important.

JB- Oh, okay.

DF- You want to earn the 50,000.

JB- Right.

DF- Here's your opportunity to ear the 50,000.

JB- I'd damn sure like to.

DF- Well, lets talk about this a little bit.

JB- Okay.

DF- Let me remind you the next day Linda came to see you, the next day.

JB- After that?

DF- Yeah.

JB- After Ada died?

DF- Yeah, do you remember the conversation you had with Linda? You told Linda to get everybody together to get their stories straight.

JB- Mmmm, boy, I don't remember that.

DF- Well, no, I mean you said it.

JB- Okay, yeah, I'm trying to think, yeah.

DF- You said it, you acknowledged it, I have the reports here. Jim, I'm not going to pull any bull shit.

JB- No, no, right, right, right.

DF- And as Jay said, you were in jail, you have the perfect alibi.

JB- Right.

DF- You could have influenced somebody.

JB- No.

DF- I'm not saying you ordered it, you may have influenced somebody, cause you even said that the next day.

JB- Right, see I told Linda, don't be harassing her, you know.

DF- Okay, but don't you remember when you found out Ada died you told Linda to get everybody together to get their stories straight?

JB- That I don't remember anymore.

DF- Well you did, you acknowledged it, and so did Linda.

JB- I probably did.

DF- I don't want to see people not responsible go to jail.

JB- Right.

DF- We need to get our memories back.

JB- I'm trying.

DF- I want this..

JB- Rena's the one who told me.

DF- What did she tell you?

JB- It was the next day, she told me that Ada was dead, she had her head cut off.

DF- Do you know what happened to Ada?

JB- Yeah, she was stabbed, I seen it on the news last night.

DF- So why do you think Eddie didn't do this?

JB- I just can't see Ed. He was such a nice guy. Everybody loved Ed.

DF- Oh, Jim, let's face it, Ed beat the shit out of people.

JB- Oh yeah, I mean..

DF- That's not being a nice guy, plus Ed hated snitches.

JB- Well everybody hates snitches, really.

DF- The fact of the matter is Ada was a snitch because of what she done to you.

JB- I don't think anybody held that against her.

DF- Jim, you just said Linda was mad as hell.

JB- I thought you were talking about Ed. We were all friends, she brought my whole family food.

DF- Well..

JB- I was going to jail, cause there's nothing going to happen, you know.

DF- Linda told everybody Ada turned you in for having sex with Helen.

JB- Ada never turned me in, I was brought back for drinking, and it was perfectly legal at that time.

DF- For what?

JB- With a 16 year old, right.

DF- Right.

JB- You guys know Ada would bring her to bed with us, when Linda was gone.

JR- But it's not legal in Wisconsin, and that's why Bill Hammes held it over you.

JB- That ain't why I get revoked, I got brought back for drinking.

JR- That's why he held you.

JB- No, I was brought back for drinking.

JR- That's why he held you for so long.

DF- Well, Linda put it in everybody's mind that Ada put you in jail.

JB- Okay.

DF- They even got her to recant, we have the notarized paper. After you told them to get their stories straight, what did you and Linda talk about?

JB- I wanted her to tell me Jack did it, cause I was going to turn his ass in.

DF- What if you told you it was Eddie, would you have turned him in?

JB- No, I wouldn't.

DF- What if she told you it was Dennis Mickelson?

JB- Now, by God there was, he used to hang around down there. I don't remember him though.

DF- What if she told you it was him?

JB- I would have turned him in.

DF- What did she say about Dennis?

JB- I'm trying to think. I don't remember her mentioning Dennis. I really don't.

DF- Jim, do you feel some liability on this whole thing?

JB- No, not one bit. I'll take a lie detector or any damn thing.

DF- Okay, but that's a simple question.

JB- Okay, I had nothing what so ever, I mean if had been Edward, then no I wouldn't have turned him in. But I wanted her to say it was Jack, I really did. At that point I would have turned her in too.

DF- What motive would Jack have had to kill Ada, if Ada was keeping you in jail?

JB- Right.

DF- Okay, why would he kill Ada if that means you can't get out?

JB- Oh, it would make damn sure I wouldn't get out. If she's said "Jack" I'd of turned them both in. Now that other guy, I can't remember his name.

DF- No, we won't worry about him right now.

JB- Okay, but…

DF- We'll deal with him later. So why would Jack go and do all those things and try and get Ada to change her story, to get you out of jail?

JB- Uh..

DF- Do you think Linda would kill for you?

JB- I don't think she did it, I think Jack did it, to keep me in jail and get in her good graces.

DF- How would Jack and Linda go about doing this?

JB- That's what I'm not, see Jack was a friend, but Ada wouldn't have let him in.

DF- Let's talk a little more about how Linda paid Jack.

JB- Right.

DF- And how she worked this out. Jim, what do you know about that?

JB- Well she never came out and said so, but I had this suspicion.

DF- You were damn mad about that party, it was like a celebration of Jim being in jail, right?

JB- Yes it was.

DF- What did your boys tell you about the next day, cleaning out the cars?

JB- Wait a minute, wait a minute, Jack killed a turtle, they were cleaning the blood out of the trunk or something.

DF- I don't think Jack did it, I think Ed did that, actually.

JB- Edward?

DF- I think Eddie killed the turtle. So why were they cleaning?

JB- I don't know.

DF- Was Linda mad when you had sex with Ada?

JB- She never knew about it.

DF- Well she did when Bill Hammes came down on you.

JB- She was never mad about it.

DF- She was okay with you having sex with Ada and Helen?

JB- I never had to explain…

DF- Did you have sex with Rena?

JB- No.

DF- Do you think Eddie's involved?

JB- You think he was?

DF- I really do Jim. There's an awful lot of things that point at Eddie. Why on one certain night he have a blackout? Why would Eddie bring a bloody shirt home and wash it the night Ada died?

JB- I don't know.

DF- Well these are facts, Jim.

JB- Right.

DF- Maybe Ada wasn't the pillar of the community.

JB- She didn't deserve that shit.

DF- Her heart was big.

JB- She's come around with that chicken and bring food, that how Bobby Fort go so mad. It was his money she was spending on us. She was supposed to pay his bills or something.

DF- Probably.

JB- She took antiques out of his house and bought us beer and shit.

DF- Now Jim, I'm not pointing fingers, but I'm going to say the Linda Erickson group, doesn't it makes sense that someone in that group killed her?

JB- I uh, they never told me.

DF- Do you think Eddie would?

JB- If he was drunk enough, probably.

DF- You can't just see anybody going and killing Ada?

JB- No, I can't. Not for the hell of it, no.

DF- Come on Jim, maybe it didn't start out that way, but it sure ended up, let's say they were going to punish Ada for something.

JB- Right.

DF- We're going to wrap this up, okay if we come back and talk to you soon?

JB- Definitely, I'll take a lie detector test too.

DF- Well, we haven't talked about that at this point. You'd love to pin this on Jack, wouldn't you?

JB- Jack and Linda both, I wouldn't give s shit about them.

This concludes their first interview with Jim. The investigators went to question his son, Danny, who was in jail, and then came back to Jim on the 4th of October, 2006. This is a short interview that is only 31 pages and it is posted in it's entirety on the blog as well. The blog post is titled "I want that money."

Denny and Jay are in the home of Albert Bolstad, in Lacrosse. Jim is very eager to talk to them.

JB- Well I went and spoke to my son, Danny, what was it, Thursday night?

DF- Mmmhmmm.

JB- I said Danny, damn it tell them the truth. I told him about Edward and the bloody clothes, and the trunk of the car. I've tracked down Dennis Mickelson, he's in prison, I didn't know if you guys knew that.

DF- I did not know he was in prison.

JB- He's in prison, I tracked him to Black River Falls. I've been calling and calling and I never, Edward never told me he did it.

DF- All right.

JB- Rod Carpenter, that's his name. He was always at the Labor Temple and he stayed with Ada at night. He'd go over there about 11 or 12 at night. so he had a place to stay.

DF- Who?

JB- Over to Ada's. And his name is Rod Carpenter. Do you have any information on him?

DF- Yeah, I think he's been interviewed.

JB- Well he was always bragging about how much money she had in them things. Down at the Labor Temple. Two weeks after Ada got killed, he was at the Labor Temple hollering at Junior Benson and Edward, cause they had kicked the shit out of him for stalking my sister. He was hollering at them "I'll kill you like I killed Ada!". And he was bragging about it, that he killed Ada.

DF- Mmmhmm.

JB- Now this here's a hell of a good lead.

DF- Hmm.

JB- Now why would he be bragging about killing her?

Murder and Deceit

JR- Did Danny tell you about Rod Carpenter?

JB- A little bit, I say "I'm going to get that 50,000." Danny says he knows Rod too, not very good though.

DF- What did Danny talk about?

JB- Danny said," Dad I don't remember it was so long ago."

DF- Jim, how do you see yourself, as kind the hierarchy of the family? They look to you..

JB- Not really. So Danny didn't even talk about the reward. He says "Dad, I don't know nothing." And I says "I might tell you some of the stuff, but not everything, you might go after the reward", you know kind of joking.

DF- Mmmhmm.

JB- I sure could use that 50,000.

DF- Mmmhmm.

JB- Well that's all I could find out, Rod Carpenter.

DF- Let's say that, that Linda and Jack, and your theory.

JB- Right, that's my theory.

DF- How do you think they'd done that?

JB- She's just pay him and he would go over and do that.

DF- Alone?

JB- Why not?

DF- What about Ed?

JB- You know this Rod Carpenter, that's my theory.

DF- Hmm.

JB- Well that's the best I can come up with for now. I want this settled too, Ada was a good friend.

DF- Was Ed afraid of Jack Nissalke?

JB- He wasn't afraid of nobody.

DF- Was Linda afraid of Jack?

JB- Not that I know of.

JR- Are you afraid of anybody, Jim?

JB- I ain't afraid of nobody.

JR- I mean Jack or Linda, Jim.

JB- I know I ain't afraid of nobody.

JR- Mickelson?

JB- Nope. I want that money.

DF- Cause if you want that money you keep checking.

JB- I'm going to keep working on it. I'll keep checking cause I want that money.

DF- Well take care Jim. Let us hear from you.

JB- Anything I come up with you're going to get, cause I want that damn money.

DF- All right.

JB- If it's Rod, I get the money right?

JR- (laughs)

JB- If it turns out to be Rod' it's mine, right?

Well, it turned out to not be Rod. MacLean and Gort were having orgasms over this guy. James Bolstad would clearly say anything they wanted him to. They put Bolstad in jail with Linda and Jack, as co-conspirators to fit their 'theory', that criminal mastermind, Jimmy Bolstad, got his girl friend, Linda Parrish(Erickson), to hire Jack Nissalke to kill Ada Senenfelder out of revenge over what she had done to Jim. They presented Jim the same deal as Linda, roll on Jack, say what they wanted, or life in prison. He took their deal and is free today. He doesn't want to talk to me. By the way, they offered Jack a deal too. He refused it, because he happens to be innocent, and true to their threats, he did get life in prison.

After Jack was in prison, the legal system had to honor the deal they made Linda and Jim. In order to do that, they had to dismiss the murder indictment against them. MacLean filed the papers on July 9, days after he'd won his trial. The Judge Jeffery Thompson signed them on October 27, 2009. I have the document posted on my blog. The reasons he gives in the dismissal are the actual reason for doing this.

He lists four reasons for letting them go:

1. Fair and impartial trial.
The Judge notes that members on the Grand Jury had formed opinions about Jack Nissalke from the news and rumors around town. One juror was biased against Jack and told the panel that Jack had robbed their family and was certainly capable of murder. The juror was dismissed but the others got hear this 'opinion'.

2. Sufficiency of evidence.
Here the Judge chides MacLean for getting a legal indictment based on inadmissible evidence. MacLean told the Grand Jury that Jim Bolstad called Linda Parrish and told the party goers to commit murder, even though there is no evidence of such. The Judge goes on to note that the lack of any real, admissible evidence, only hearsay evidence, leads him to believe that Jim and Linda are both not guilty. I wonder where that leaves Jack? He notes that 'bad acts' were committed in the court room. He details them as prejudice, confusion of issues, misleading the jury, and a wasting of time.

3. Creating and nurturing and atmosphere of fear.
Here the Judge says that MacLean and Gort were just trying to scare the jurors when they informed them of extra security was provided because the 'gang' of Jimmy Bolstad were so dangerous, they might be in danger. They went home thinking that Jack Nissalke was Jim and Linda's 'snitch' killer, and woe to them if they didn't lock them all up forever. He goes on to say that the DA told them these were just 'bad' people and never presented credible. admissible evidence to match up his lies.

4. Curable defect.

Lastly, the Judge shows the cumulative effect of all this amounts to being unfair and biased. There's a saying that a DA can indict a ham sandwich, if he wants to, he's just not supposed to. The only thing a Grand Jury in this country hears is what a DA tells them. A defense lawyer can not present opposing evidence. Our system depends on people in the DA's Office to be honorable and fair. When they are not, justice is not carried out. The Judge says the 'cure' is to dismiss these false charges.

This is after they have used it to send an innocent man to prison.

Meeting John Senenfelder

When I went back to Winona in September, 2010, I had a laundry list of people to talk to that were willing and eager by this point. I spent my days at The Acoustic Coffee Shop, where I set up shop. I had a make shift office there, combined with great food, coffee, beer, and WIFI. People would wait in chairs like a Doctor's office. One such person I was urged to try and speak with was John Senenfelder, Ada's husband. The *Winona Daily News* had published an article about him, showing him in his wheelchair, both legs gone, waving at the cars passing in front of his house. It seems they tricked him to talking to them about his car waving so they could pepper him with uncomfortable questions about Ada, and his prison sentence for molestation. I was convinced he would not want to talk to me. Besides, I already had plenty of folks who did want to. One day at Ron Nissalke's house, he mentioned that Harley Howell, a nearby neighbor, had a son Gary, who died mysteriously, had told him that Bobby Fort had Ada killed. I had the interview, but did want to talk to Harley to see if there was any more to the story as there usually is. Ron called up Harley and said we could come talk to him the next afternoon. Ron came and drove there at our appointed time. Together we went down a near by alley, as it seemed Harley spent his afternoons in his open garage that faced the alley and wanted to meet there, instead of inside his house. He was there waiting with plastic lawn chairs just inside the garage. We sat down as Harley and Ron lit cigarettes and we began to chat. Harley seemed to be mid to late 70's, thin and very animated. It pleased him we were there, and I briefly told him what I was doing. He told me matter of fact that Jack was framed and he knew Bobby Fort had Ada killed. Other than that, he offered nothing new. We talked for a good 20 minutes, when I mentioned the John S. story in the paper. Harley surprised us by allowing that he and John are friends and John usually comes by the garage every afternoon. Harley said that we had just missed him. Harley said he and John were long time friends and he is reserved, quiet, and doesn't like to talk. I asked if he would ask John S. if he would talk to me. Harley said he would, but seriously doubted he would, especially after the paper "fucked him over like they did". I persisted and Harley said he would ask. Ron and I left there thinking, well we had tried.

The next day, Harley called Ron who then called me. It seems John would at least meet me, but any talk about the past was off limits. Ron picked me up at the coffee shop and we felt some excitement, why, I wasn't sure. As we turned up the alley, we could see the garage was open and sure enough, Harley sat in one of 3 chairs, and there was John S., in his wheelchair, smoking a small cigar. I was nervous, and so was he. We exchanged an awkward handshake and I pulled up a chair on his right side. Ron and Harley lit up and moved a few feet away. I tried my best to tell him as gently as I could that I was grateful he consented to meet me, and did not want to cause him pain. He nodded in silence and stared out into the alley way as cars came by. It was certainly a busy alley. The sun shone on our faces as I outlined the book I was writing, and just wanted some back ground on Ada. There had to be more that I had. What was she like as a wife? I tried to start a conversation but was going no where until I asked him if he was from Winona? John S. replied no, he was from Iowa. I told him I was in Iowa recently to visit some of my cousins for the first time. He seemed to perk up just a little underneath his shell and asked me where? I told him and we started to talk.

He came here in the late 1960's after a huge storm had knocked down a lot of trees. He got work cleaning up the town, and stayed on. He eventually became a plumber and made "big money," as he characterized it several times. I asked him how he met Ada, and he softly replied that it was "through friends." I asked him to rate his marriage to her and he said there were many good times. I knew that Ada was married to Casmir Flak, and there were 3 children when he married her. I never knew how Casmir died until I asked John S. "Cancer," he replied. I was encouraged now and asked what Ada was like? He glanced at me and said she liked to party a lot. At that point he thrust his arms down and wheeled away. I watched as he went down the alley home. I had really talked to John Senenfelder. Harley told me that he had never seen him talk so much. Ron and I left there, with me thinking I had done my share of harm to a man who seemed kind and gentle, though shielded. Something in me liked this man, a man who had been convicted of molesting his step-daughter. Just before he took off, I sensed I was losing him, and asked if I could come again to see him? He said yes.

The next day, Ron came and drove me to the alley after he had picked up the type of cigars John was smoking. It was raining lightly and the garage was closed. No John S. We planned to try the next day and about an hour before it was time, Ron called me to say "He's there right now." We drove over and gave him the cigars. He seemed very happy to see us, and this time all 4 of us just talked for a while. I made my mind up to not bring up anything serious. John S. lit up a cigar as I showed him pictures I had been taking along the river. He told me how he lost his legs. He was in a boat fishing when a blood vessel burst in his lower back. He said it felt like a bolt of electricity. The problem stemmed from his diabetes. They had to take his legs. I asked him if he cooked for himself and how he managed at home. His daughters come to take him shopping and to check on him. Most days he is content to be alone, wave at the people passing by, and visit with Harley. Several times he wheeled into the alley and I asked if he was going? He smiled and said no. He just likes to move around a little. He stayed for over an hour. I told him I was leaving for a few days to see Jack and some other business in Minneapolis. I asked if Saturday was a day to see him again and ask some of the questions I needed for the book. He said sure. Before he left, he wheeled right up next to me and stuck out his hand. "Thanks, for the cigars." I told him that it was Ron who bought them and he thanked Ron as well. A few days later, Ron and I were coming back from seeing Jack. He told me that the day before that Harley had called Ron because John S. was wondering where I was. Ron reminded Harley that I said I would be back on Saturday. Evidently, John S. was eager to see me now. I wish I had that effect on everybody.

Saturday rolled around and so did the clouds. It rained all afternoon. Still we went over to closed garage just to see. Sunday was my last day in Winona. Ron and Tasha (a friend) came to get me. As we drove up the alley, John S. was waiting in front of the closed garage. We parked quickly as Ron got Harley from the house and we set up the chairs. Harley came out with refreshments as Tasha took pictures. I signaled John S. to move to the side of the garage so we could have a private chat. When we were out of earshot of the others, I told him about my visit with Jack in prison. In a clearer and stronger voice, he asked he how was he doing? He allowed that prison was no picnic. I mustered up my courage and asked him if the documents I had were right, and that he never had sex with his step-daughter. He turned and looked me in the eye and said "Ada framed me." I asked him why? He replied that she wanted to be with Bobby Fort and wanted rid of him. When I asked his opinion of Fort, he muttered "He's a crook, a criminal." I then inquired if he thought Jack killed his wife. Very calmly he told me that he knew Jack did not kill Ada, that he was certain Bobby Fort had her killed. He said that he met a man a the Labor Temple who claimed Fort paid him to kill her. Very soon after that, the man moved to the Twin Cities. He couldn't remember his name. I sat there thinking that if the justice system had any real desire to solve her death, there were plenty of real people willing to say that without a doubt Bobby Fort, not Jack Nissalke, was responsible for her murder. I tried to imagine the jury from Jack's trial listening to this man in his wheelchair. I sipped a beer as John S. drank one of

Harley's Pepsis, right next to the man whose son is serving life in prison for the death of this man's wife. The day after I left, Ron stopped by John S.'s home and gave him a bag of unshelled walnuts. He enjoys feeding squirrels.

MacLean's "Star"

One of the most improbable witnesses against Jack was Rena Bambenek. MacLean had tons of statements from this woman from 1985 through the 1990's. After reading them, he couldn't decide to arrest her or put her on the witness stand. After several interviews, they let her decide. Rena, who was drooling over the 50k, was also giving the impression she was hiding something. MacLean knew this too, and offered her a deal: Help frame Jack, or go to jail. This was no different that the tactic he used on others, except, Rena was *very* motivated to comply. For months, they coached her in a motel miles away from Winona. Taxpayers had to support this very important witness. The question was, witness to what? Rena was a single mom, who lived next door to the Bolstads. She claimed to have stayed home the night of the party and Ada's killing. She admitted being at Ada's house after Jack, Linda, and the rest were meeting with Ada and the probation man. She and Dennis Mickelson picked up the chicken Ada gave them, and left the unthawed ham on the table, with the promise to return. The package of ham was still there when they discovered Ada's body. She said she didn't kill Ada or witness her murder. She also said she didn't attend the party at Linda's house. So what did she witness? She took the stand and said she saw Jack Nissalke with a cut, bleeding hand, wrapped in a towel. She claimed Steve Pagel was helping Jack look for a flashlight. Steve took the stand and said it never happened. Everybody at the party said Jack never left, but Ed Bolstad did. Where did the cut hand story come from? About a month after Ada died, Jack and Ed tried to break into a motorcycle shop, unsuccessfully. Jack cut his hand then, The cops looked at Jack's hand the morning after Ada was murdered and found no cuts. They did find some on Ed Bolstad. Now, did Rena get confused in her timeline over the 20 years? I doubt it. She never mentions this in any of her statements back then. MacLean used a method with some of the witnesses called "new memories." With the help of suggestion, they would "help" some of the witnesses with a new memory, one that didn't exist before. When questioned under oath, Rena admitted that some of her "new memories" were "false memories". What in the hell is anything false being admitted in a court of law? Why would she willingly lie under oath? Was it just a shot at the money? Maybe. To answer that, let's go back to 1985.

No one was interviewed more times in 1985 about Ada's murder than Rena Bambenek. She seemed to be a link to everyone from Ed and Jim Bolstad to Bobby Fort. She was in love with Ed and was heartbroken he was also having sex with Ada when he spent the night at her house. Right after the murder she gave Sgt. T O Nyseth over 30 pages of testimony on July 19, 1985. She said that after Ed helped tear down a wall over at Lee Campbell's house, he washed clothes and had cleaned up. She drove him around that evening and said Ed was very nervous. His parents finally came an got him and he ran to their car and slumped in the back seat. Rena got a call about 6 p.m. from Thelma Nation to come over and get Ed. Vicki Wicka came over to babysit Allyson, Rena's daughter. After getting gas she pulled up and Ed ran out and jumped in the car and told her to drive to Lewiston. They stopped at the Golfview Liquor and Ed bought a 6 pack of Blatz beer. Ed seemed upset and couldn't stop talking about Ada. He admitted she was a nice person, but she got what was coming for narcing on people. After driving around in the country for a while, they stopped at the Rustic Bar in Lewiston. Rena got a gin and sour, while Ed drank brandy and coke. Ed didn't talk much and they left after about a half hour and drove to Linda Parrish's apartment. Linda was there with Raymond, Danny, June, and Roger Bolstad, Laurie and Jack Nissalke. There were no children there. Until about 10 p.m., they talked about Ada and who could have done it. Most of them were not worried about being suspects as they had been there at Linda's, except for Ed who left and came back. He declared "We were all here at a party!" Rena got June to drive her home after 10 p.m.. She noticed that the driver's door on Ed's brown Mercury was not acting properly earlier. When she asked Ed about the damage, he said he didn't know. Rena said Ada was pleased that everyone knew she was having sex with Ed and called him the new "boss" since Jim was in jail. Rena knew that Ada was supplying Ed with Bobby Fort's money for beer at their parties. The last party was on June 2, days before Ada was murdered. Ada called people to her house and took a hundred dollar bill out and asked some to buy the liquor. Roger, Ed, and Jack went to Stockton and came back with a half barrel of beer, and bottles of Windsor and Kessler's whiskey. They kept the change and split it up between several of them, and headed back to the Bolstads' apartment where Ada and the others were getting the party going. Quite a number of friends came and went as the liquor flowed freely. About 1 am, Ed took out a hatchet and began to show it to people. He said that Bobby Benson had stolen it from K-Mart and given it to him. While in the kitchen, Rena saw Ed take out $600 he had received from Ada. Linda then asked Ada for some money to help Jim get out of jail, but Ada said that's all she had except for a check at home. Ada promised Linda to help her wash clothes the next day. Linda then asked if Ada would talk to Jim's probation officer and she agreed. The group had stolen Ada's radio and bicycle in retaliation for her snitching on Jim, and now they promised to return them if she recanted. The party ended and Rena went home, next door.

In this very extensive interview, Rena barely mentions Jack's name. As she describes the brands of beer, whiskey, the exact times, and full names, she doesn't mention Jack having a cut hand, wrapped in a bloody towel, looking for a flashlight.

In January of 1986, the police were called to Thomas and Lori Danzeisen's house. Rena had accused Gary Casper of having an affair with Lori and in a drunken rage began to beat the daylights out of him. When police arrived, they found Casper, dazed, sitting in a living room chair. His glasses were broken and his shirt was ripped to shreds. He didn't want to press charges, but only asked them to keep Rena from him. They found Rena, wildly drunk in the kitchen, also stating she wasn't pressing charges. The Danzeisens asked Rena to leave their house; she went into the living room and began to scream at Casper. The officer tried to calm her down, and offered her a taxi. She refused and they offered her a ride in the squad car home. She yelled at Casper and said she needed to talk to him. He sat in silence which made her even madder. The officers once again offered her a ride, to which Rena told them she would drive herself home. The cautioned her that they would arrest her for DWI. Rena insisted on speaking her mind to Gary and sat down on the kitchen table. They arrested her and tried to get her to stand up. She wrapped her legs around some chair legs and struggled and fought them back. They finally got handcuffs on her and began to pull her through the house. She fought like a wild cat and hung on to pieces of furniture and began to break apart the things she passed. Outside the house was another giant struggle until they got her in the squad car. Rena would not cooperate with the booking officers and they dispatched social services to get her daughter and take her into foster care.

When Rena found out Ed was sleeping with Ada, people say she was beside herself with anger and a broken heart. Experts I have talked to believe that some of the 33 stab wounds came from a woman, as they are shallow. They also think that part of the circumstances for her murder resulted out of passion. Later in August of 86, Casper would tell police that Rena told him she helped Ed wash his bloody clothes after he killed Ada Senenfelder.

Casper was afraid of the Bolstads and expressed fear for knowing this. In 2006, the police would again visit Casper and have him recall dating Rena and her confession to washing Ed's bloody clothes. Only Rena knows what Rena knows, and presently there's no reward money for a new story. However, in her quest to hide what she really does know, and the shot at a lot of money, Rena Bambenek became a pawn for MacLean and Gort, and helped put the wrong man behind bars.

The Blog

A few years ago, I had heard of blogs, but never read one. I really didn't have an idea what they contained or why they were gaining popularity. I had no thought that "blogger" would soon be on my business cards. A year earlier, my youngest son, and collaborator on the fiction I write, Josh, started telling me that I should create a blog so people could see what I was writing. Others had wondered why I hadn't and I kept it in the back of my mind. In the spring of 2010, I had finished another book and was busy researching Jack's story. I thought it was a perfect time to explore this venue. One problem: I didn't know how. I texted another son, Matt, who gave me a web address, and said it was rather simple. He was right. I toyed with several names that were already taken, and settled on my second book, which was my first novel. By trial and error I got used to the format and posted it on Facebook, all of which costs nothing.

I quickly discovered that a blog is like a newspaper —and I ran out of things to report. I shifted to Jack's story and soon had 100 readers per posting. 100! Wow, I thought that was great. To me it was like standing up in a bar and ranting and all 100 strangers listening. Soon, the plight of Jack Nissalke dominated the blog as I became more obsessed with freeing him. The number soon reached 1,000, then 5,000, 10,000, sometimes a little more. I couldn't believe it. Each month, I learned new things about how to blog. One of the first things I soon encountered, was high praise and utter contempt. I had no idea if this would help Jack or not, but I sure found out how strong people's opinions are. The first real police documents I got, I painstakingly copied them and posted them. I was accused of making this up and there was a call for me to scan the entire document and let them see what I was "hiding." I didn't have a scanner and I thought it wouldn't matter anyway, they could claim that I manufactured it. I was heavily criticized for typing errors, so I found the spell-check button the blog has and got a spelling-error free post. I eventually borrowed my son John Jr.'s scanner, not to pacify the critics, but so I wouldn't have so much to type. The documents looked cool, but the critics kept finding more injustices and this came from the comments themselves. At times there were wars between readers and I had to remove them. On one trip I found out the judges were reading the blog. Winona began to refer to it as "The Blog". As in "Have you read the crazy shit on the blog today?" Early in the blog, Chuck MacLean left town, and later so did Tom Gort, and I was encouraged to step up my news on it. I wish I could take credit for their leaving, but there were other factors troubling them besides me. I posted my phone number and email trying to get more people to tell me what they knew. I soon got the gamut of solid information to a steady diet of harassment. My phone still gets several restricted calls, while most are hang ups, there have been some voices threatening me. I have learned that the creeps are too chicken to actually do anything, and besides, I live in California! One week the blog had over 190,000 hits and I am still amazed at how far Jack's story has spread.

Laurie Nissalke

One person who was at the party at Linda's house was one of Jack's sisters, Laurie. Laurie was 17 at the time and was dating Roger Bolstad. Laurie knew Ada and was at most of the parties the Bolstads hosted. Over the years, Laurie was questioned aggressively. As Jack's sister, and being friends with the same people being questioned and under suspicion, the investigators insisted that she had to have known something. Laurie's account stays the same over the entire 20 years. She doesn't know who killed Ada. She knows it wasn't her brother as he was at the same party as she was. She was called a liar in some of the interviews as they said she must be covering for Jack or the real killers. I have gotten to know Laurie very well during this journey. If she knew anything about something as serious as murder, she wouldn't be able to keep it a secret. Laurie is a kind, loving, gentle soul who ran with a bad crowd when she was young. In fact, most of the people who were teens or older at the party were not bad people. There is no way that many of them could keep a secret as big as a conspiracy to commit murder. Kids will talk.

The following is the abbreviated account of the statement Laurie gave on 9-29-06. The entire interview is on the blog. The investigators pick Laurie up at her parents' house and drive her around, a favorite tactic then. SB is Scott Bestul, the investigator, and LN is Laurie. It is transcribed by Sarah Berg. There is another investigator from the Twin Cities named John Seery, referred to as JS.

SB- Why don't you have a seat in the car, Laurie, so we're not competing with the noise?
LN- Oh I seen it in the paper yesterday, so I figured I got questioned back then, they'll be coming again, so okay.
SB- I'm going to give you one these flyers, there's an awful lot of money out there this time around.

LN- Yeah, it is.

SB- You gave a

LN- I sure could use that money, I wish I knew something.

JS- You gave a few reports back in the day, a couple of different things you said. And we just want to go through your, what you remember surrounding the death of Ada.

LN- I don't remember anything other than being scared I was being investigated for a murder, and wondering why we were being investigated, and knowing there were some weird stories being said about her. Like the guys were doing funny stuff with her, like there were parties and she would get drunk, and I don't know. I've learned more about my remembrance about it reading that newspaper article. I can't even remember that specifically.

JS- Have you had any contact with anybody since we started this case this week?

LN- No.

JS- No one called you?

LN- No

JS- and said don't say a thing?

LN- No nobody.

JS- Well lets see if we can get you to remember some things, like the party at Linda Erickson's apartment.

LN- Okay.

JS- Do you remember that?

LN- I do remember that, yeah.

JS- Do you remember who all was there?

LN- I mean I can't remember, yeah there was a party that night. I don't remember who all was there. I know me and my boyfriend at the time, Roger.

JS- Roger Bolstad?

LN- Yep. I think my brother Jack was there, but I'm not for sure, God, I can't remember that night specifically. I think it was in her apartment behind the hospital.

JS- Mmmmhmm.

LN- I mean that was a big deal being investigated for a murder back then.

JS- There were some information, some reports your brother Jack was involved.

LN- Pardon me?

JS- Someone there, there's been some information out there you were confronted with someone saying that Jack was involved in that.

LN- I've never heard that.

JS- Okay, that was an emotional time for you back then?

LN- I've been emotional my whole life. Looking back on that time frame, I was with the wrong people. I wish I knew something, maybe I could have went another direction and may be in a different spot right now. I stayed with Roger for 10 years.

JS- You knew him quite well.

LN- Oh yeah.

JS- You knew he held court?

LN- What?

JS- You knew he held court at some point in those...

LN- He held court?

JS- in those ten years didn't you?

LN- What's "held court" mean?

JS- The Bolstad clan would hold court with people that had done something wrong to their family.

LN- I never heard that term.

JS- Do you have a nickname that everybody, that you called him?

LN- Roger?

JS- Yeah.

LN- The only one I ever heard was Bullwinkle.

SB- We've heard other people talking about that family of people associated with them holding court.

LN- No, in fact the friends I hung around with, the Bolstads, nobody felt scared, I don't have any facts to prove that.

JS- Did they all carry knives back then?

LN- Not that I knew of.

SB- We talked to Roger yesterday and he said he carried a knife all the time back then.

LN- Well then maybe he did, I don't know.

SB- Everybody carried knives.

LN- I never seen them.

SB- Describe your relationship with Ada.

LN- I didn't have a relationship with her. I don't ever remember talking to her.

SB- Do you remember going over to her house for some chicken?

LN- No.

SB- I'm reading a statement here, that you and a bunch of people went over to her house and fried up some chicken.

LN- Really?

JS- Yeah. Are you telling us everything you know? Or are you, I still think you are holding back a little.

LN- There's nothing I know. Really. If I did know something, I would tell you. I just know it scares me that somebody would do something like that, that there still out there on the street.

JS- Try to bring back something that will refresh your memory, there was a morning, it would have been the day Ada was found, her body. You guys after a party at Linda Erickson's went to the Country Kitchen for breakfast. Roger was real drunk and passed out.

LN- I can't remember anything.

JS- I would have been after you guys were drinking at Linda's.

LN- Yeah.

JS- Do you remember the Linda Erickson party?

LN- No, I can't remember, I really can't.

Murder and Deceit

JS- Part of our investigation now, there's a reason we started investigating, opened the case back up, you know, modern technology, we do things different now.

LN- Right.

JS- DNA evidence.

LN- Good.

JS- The crime scene was a mess, there was a lot we recovered from that.

LN- Yeah.

JS- Didn't you guys have a meeting to blame the Forts and take blame away from the Bolstads?

LN- No one ever told me "this is what you can say, and this is what you can't say." No one ever said that to me.

JS- But you were at that meeting.

LN- What meeting?

JS- The one Linda called to get everyone's story straight.

LN- That ain't what Linda said and that's the truth.

JS- So we're going to get the people who did this, and the people who are holding back and aiding these people.

LN- That's good, I mean..

JS- It's more than one person who actually committed the crime. There are people who aren't telling and that's just as bad as doing the crime.

LN- That's true, but I'm not going to sit here and make it look like I'm aiding and helping some one.

JS- It's tough. What we want you to tell us is tough. You're going to be reluctant, but it's time for the truth to come out.

LN- I can take a lie detector test right now. I can get up on the stand and raise my right hand and swear I'm not lying. I swear to God.

JS- I hope not. Cause there's a reason we came to you first, we figured you would tell the truth.

LN- I did tell you the truth, from what I remember.

JS- I hope we don't have to come back here after we learn some things differently.

LN- You can come back as many times as you want, that's the truth. I didn't do it, and I don't know who did it.

JS- We're not saying you did. She was brutally stabbed, 33 times.

LN- That's so mean.

JS- If you found out your brother did it, would you protect him?

LN- No way, you gotta face up in this world.

JS- Just so you know, we're taking this very seriously, OK?

The Innocence Movement

There has never been a perfect legal system. Throughout history man has devised systems to make a fair arrangement for citizens to live by. How to punish crime has always been a continuing experiment. Each part of the globe has had great success and failure to capture the correct balance between too lenient and too harsh. Usually it has come down to a few people or even a person in power's viewpoint.

America has been one of the success stories as we evolve into a champion of human rights and a refuge that the oppressed from all over the planet would risk life and to kiss the pavement on US. soil. Our country has always made mistakes. However, because of our ideals, we normally do not enjoy dwelling on those and either learn from them or ignore them. In our 234 year history, We have on occasion put the wrong person in prison—or even executed an innocent man. We were normally assured this was as rare as seeing Halley's comet and wouldn't happen again. Writers would tell of how great a framework of laws and people assigned to manage them, and how a person (now called a case) would simply fall through a crack. There was really nothing you could do. We accepted this as the rare exception, and reasoned it was a small price to pay for the title of the great Nation on earth.

That being the state of affairs, I began to wonder why in 2010, as I walked down this path, were there now so many "cases"?

The Innocence Project has attracted national attention. As Barry Scheck has led a movement that is in every state to free the innocent. Free the innocent? What were they doing there in the first place? Did the system just suddenly just "break down"? What happened? Why hasn't there been more of an outcry before? The Innocence Project is one of the most well known, with the same agenda. At no cost to a person, they will test the old DNA from their case to see it matches the victim to the crime. In many instances, evidence has been destroyed (as in Jack's case) and there is very little hope anything can be done. At this writing, 256 human beings were exonerated by IP and let go. To me, that seems like a high number. Some of the exonerated were incarcerated over 20 years. As present, there is no way to tell how many there are behind bars that did not commit the crime they were convicted of. The legal system is certainly doing an aggressive job arresting and convicting criminals. Surely that is what our tax dollars were supposed to do. Why are there any innocent people being sentenced by a court? If you take a look at IP's website, and click on state by state, the ones being exonerated are not for petty crimes.

The felony is the top-tier of crime, composed of various degrees of murder, rape, arson, armed robbery and grand theft. These are violent crimes. What does that have to do with this?

Prosecutors are under the most pressure from voters to close these cases. Unsolved crimes of a violent nature make pesky headlines. Press conferences make the evening news. When an arrest is made, everybody is glued to the TV as if their football team just scored. They got the bad guy. Sometimes when they have to let the guy go, it is conveniently printed on page 9 and doesn't make the evening news. If the suspect, which is now referred to as the "alleged" killer, rapist, is kept behind bars, the first step is an arraignment, where the DA simply tells the judge, "he did it" and shows a few items of evidence quickly to the judge. The judge is very busy judging us and wants to move on so he is out of there by 5:00 p.m., as the court doesn't pay the judge's overtime. He almost always agrees with the DA and tells the "suspect" what he is charged with, sets the bail the DA suggests, and hits his desk with a wooden hammer.

If the "suspect" is not wealthy, the problem now is mostly financial. A court appointed lawyer who gets a stuck with him pays a jail visits to deliver the bad news. The next step is to be indicted by the Grand Jury. The Grand Jury only listens to the prosecutor tell them that the "suspect" is guilty and will provide some evidence that must put it that way, or give the reason the DA thinks he is guilty. No defense is permitted at the Grand Jury hearing and almost always they trust the DA to be doing his job and give him what he wants and indictment. Indictment literally means a formal charge or accusation of a crime. When the Grand Jury or indictment process began that is what it was intended, nothing more than being accused of a crime. Now the headlines boom and Joe Doe is indicted! The next day! Suspects now indicted for murder! In the minds of most folks, innocent people don't get INDICTED for crimes they did not commit. The fact they are only being accused of a crime never enters decent people's minds. Once indicted, a conviction normally follows. TV and moves have forever changed our viewpoint of law and order. In a live courtroom seeing a person brought in handcuffs and sit on the wrong border of the law, is a familiar scene to everybody. Innocent people don't get arrested- bad guys.

Innocent people don't get a trial by jury by their peers-bad guys. We blindly trust the legal system to the point where evidence doesn't always need to be the key factor. In most minds the need for a jury is to facilitate the legal system to help find the right sentence. So where is the very breakdown? I believe it happens somewhere between the police and the prosecutors. When a mistake is made, there are two ways that can happen. It is done either honestly or dishonestly. As hard as an honest mistake is to swallow of this magnitude, how does a dishonest mistake happen? Are there crooks working at the police department and in the courthouse? Yes, but that even is not the major portion of these wrongful convictions. The legal system is a spiderweb of dents and grey areas. They are used to people pleading to something they didn't do. It is the fabric of the plea arrangement. Usually those who are wrongly accused and convicted are not pillars of society. They are almost always minor criminals who are familiar to the process when the perfect "suspect" doesn't surface, police and prosecutors become frustrated. When a less than perfect suspect gets on their radar, they go after anything and everything that would help close the case. There is nothing more than a DA running for re-election needs is to have 100% conviction or close to it. They are willing to accept that they might not have the exact person who pulled the trigger, but, if they might have been there, if they might have a reason to commit the crime, or if enough people say they think this is person is linked to the crime, well, that is fine. The person is usually hard to like and has committed other crimes. To a dishonest prosecutor, this is just one of many wonderful ways justice is meted out. He counts on an apathetic public that only likes to hear "lock up" the bad guys. We have come to expect less than stellar lawyers unless you can pay one enough. People point to OJ Simpson now, and even that his high paid lawyers, "got him off." So, if you have enough money, you can "get off" too.

This outrages me, and the only fix I know of is to fix the system. The answer would be simple. Any person wrongly convicted by a DA and a jury would have the conviction overturned. Mistakes would be costly. Upon being freed, the courts would imprison the DA and the jury would serve the sentence they handed out to the wrong person. I have been told that is too radical. However, it would ensure everyone in the process that they got the right human. Isn't that what we want?

Doubt

Webster's Dictionary says that doubt is "feeling uncertain about something." As you read this book you may still have doubt about Jack's innocence. If you read the evidence, I don't see how, but 6 months of blogging tells me different. I posted hundreds of police interviews over and over that point to other people. I uploaded the picture of Jack at Linda's so-called party. Even the actual pictures of cuts on Ed Bolstad's hand and thumb didn't prevent some from proclaiming, "I still think Jack did it!" I learned something this year I never really believed. Prejudice is hard if not almost impossible to erase. Humans always tend to believe negative things then positive. I still don't know why. I was guilty of that emotion too, when Kristal was telling me how her brother was railroaded, a voice in me, maybe a very small tiny voice whispered, "bullshit." Isn't that what they all say? I had no idea how many times I would hear this spit back at me so matter-of-factly. So, how did I become so convinced, to the point of becoming obsessed of Jack Nissalke's innocence? I almost didn't. I nearly missed it. For Several weeks Kristal told me over and over that Jack was innocent. Finally, I read the newspaper accounts. With the exception of one, the *Winona Post*, I learned Jack was a cold-blooded killer, who tortured Ada, stabbed her for hours and got away with it. They said Jack bragged about killing her and Winona walked in fear of this monster who threatened people over and over for years. Believe me, I had doubts at that point. Kristal was naïve, I thought. How could she believe her brother was Charles Manson? I closed the book in my head and went back to a screenplay I was working on. Doubt is a funny thing. Something in my head and heart told me I was wrong. This went on for a couple of months, until on impulse I asked her for Jack's address and wrote him a letter. Slowly I became aware of the dozens of people in this twenty-year-old story. At this point, I pushed my doubts and prejudice aside and strove to learn the facts of the case. This proved to be difficult as I wrote letters and made phone calls, Nobody wanted to talk about this. Ron, Jack's dad, had amassed a considerable amount of evidence and gladly shared it with me. I only had to look at a small percentage of the evidence to erase my doubts. As I finally got more and more evidence, I thought this would be easy. By and large, that has been the case. However, each week, I encounter doubt. I have accepted that I can not overcome all of it. Each week strangers see me in a coffee shop or a bar, writing. They ask me what I am doing. I cheerfully (usually). I just tell them I am a writer. "What do you write?" That is a question I try to reduce to a small sentence rather than a long explanation, as I know they are mostly curious and don't have any real interest in what I write. If they keep asking, I give them a card with the Amazon.com web address. I tell them they can see it there. I still try to refrain from seeming like a salesman with a pitch. At the bottom of my card is the blog address. If given the chance, I will try and explain the blog and briefly, ever so briefly, tell them about Jack. Most times, they act interested and promise to "check it out." Still, a good percentage roll their eyes and smile. They always say the same thing: "That's what they all say, right?" When I insist he really is innocent, they knowingly put their card in their pocket and say "bullshit," with their eyes, their face flashes a sign that cries "doubt" as they pity a person as stupid as I.

Murder and Deceit

What I Believe Happened

After spending most of a year reading everything I could get my hands on, and after personally interviewing all who would talk about Ada's murder, I have come to some conclusions.

There are some people who have studied this case in greater detail and longer than I, but not many. When I started looking at this story, I had doubts that Jack committed the murder. Once I had access to enough evidence, I knew he didn't kill Ada. Part of my thinking in the early stages, was "why would Jack kill Ada?" Now, Jack was a big guy, a tough guy back then. But as an 18 year old kid, he didn't go around killing people. Actually, the minor-league criminal crowd he was with were not into murder. Not even Ed Bolstad. However, Ed became violent when drunk and liked to stab sometimes. Unlike MacLean and Gort, I had no theory to pin this on. I only wanted to show what I found, which was Jack was innocent. After a long investigation and time to think, I do have an idea about what the evidence says. Have I solved the murder? No. Her murder will stay unsolved until someone who was in her house that night, when Ada took her last breath, wants to talk. Are there people like that still out there alive? I do think so.

The more I thought about why would Jack kill Ada, the following truths became evident. Jack barely knew Ada, he was put off by her, and she didn't care for him either. She wouldn't even let Jack in her house late at night. Jack didn't have a strong enough bond with Linda or Jim to kill for hire or for a favor. Hey Jack, wouldn't you please go kill Ada for us? No, a brutal murder like that doesn't make sense. There is no motive or direct evidence linking Jack. At trial, jilted girlfriends were giving an ever-changing story, out of hate for Jack, and the other reason was the $50,000. Then, there is that alibi and the pictures. So who did it and why?

Most crimes that are solved are done so within three days. This is when the trail is hot and more work hasn't piled up on the desk of the investigators. From day 1, the FBI, BCA and the ATF all had one suspect and only one: Bobby Fort. The only problem was Bobby was in jail and didn't actually kill her. He had other people do it. The motive as I have previously stated was after Bobby's county jail sentence was up the Feds were definitely sending him away. Bobby was going to die in a prison cell and he was terrified of that prospect. The other prospect was Bobby could roll on other bigger fish and probably end up free, but dead. The consensus between Fort, Earl Lemon, and the Bolstads was this woman is bad news. The whole town knows she is a terrible mother and a sex toy for even the lowest rung of society. They counted no one curious enough to look very deep. They were right. I do think Bobby Fort got away with murder, along with some others. The idea, that someone like Jack would end up getting blamed has to be a relief to some of them even now. Who?

Police reports show that Bobby wanted Ada gone. Informants who were with him daily for years called Bobby a dangerous man who if he wanted you gone, you were gone. There is enough evidence to show three or four people were responsible for killing Ada. The police never doubted Ed Bolstad was one of them. He had motive, his brother was going to prison on Ada's say-so, but mainly I think he was directed to act this out on order from Bobby Fort. The night of Linda's party Ed looked pensive and moody. Everyone seemed to being having fun but him. I think he counted on the pictures proving his alibi; if not, his drunk friends would cover for him being gone for awhile. He never counted on the cops showing up for a noise complaint and documenting him leaving. Ed's body language in the photos shows him in a serious frame of mind. He must leave at a set time, why? Ed, I think mainly was to be the driver to take the others to confront Ada over Bobby Fort's upcoming charges, not Jimmy Bolstad's. So, who was with him? Evidence proves Rena Bambenek knew volumes about the murder and most of the testimony. This is in spite of her supposedly being home with her daughter all night. Motive? Rena

Murder and Deceit

was insanely jealous of Ed, and was distraught over her boyfriend having sex with Ada. She was humiliated. But Rena had ties to Bobby Fort, too. After Ada's death, she and Fort drank regularly at the Labor Temple while she dated a nephew of Bobby's. Crime-scene evidence points to a woman involved, mainly the multiple stab wounds and their shallow depth. Definitely a non-professional. Who was the third or fourth person? Since the police never pursued what the FBI gave them, we may never know. Dennis Mickelson left the party, went to Rena's supposedly, and returned all sweaty, as did Ed. Albert Bolstad, who was the most violent, was also a suspect. Albert brushed off the police, but would drop hints about Bobby Fort. John Senenfelder and a host of others talked of a mysterious man Bobby hired to kill Ada. Still, Rena left the unthawed ham to have a reason for a later return after she got the chicken from Ada. We know Ada's kitchen was missing two knives. One lay across her dead body, splattered with her blood. The other was never found. We don't know if it was taken before her death or was used in her murder. After looking at the video and the photos of the scene, Ada's murder looks spontaneous and not well planned. I think it was probably an instance of manslaughter or un-pre meditated murder. However, there were plenty of reasons to think it was a hit for hire. The evidence just shows a sloppy, bloody sight that looks like it got out of hand. They ran and left Ada where she lay, not even bothering to pull her away from between the wall and bed. The neighbors heard fighting. Some neighbors saw them leave. Once the town heard the Bolstads were involved, they shut up.

The police interviewed countless people who knew nothing. They refused to believe that Bobby Fort ordered this. The three days passed and no arrests were made. Bobby got out of jail and resumed his fencing. The Bolstads continued to use the jails as a part-time home. Jack grew up and raised a family.

The 1990's: The Investigation Goes On

During this decade after Ada's unsolved murder, the investigation plodded on. Investigators continued to question an endless list of Bolstads and associates. They talked to Rena quite often and found she would add a new twist to her shifting story. Jack Nissalke was a favorite as rumors would surface that claimed "Jack did it." Most of this type of information came from old girlfriends or someone who heard something from a friend of a friend. Nonetheless, Winona kept paging their officials to answer every call and track down any rumor. Linda Parish (Erickson) was also a favorite subject for their visits. The documents were kept methodically and began to pile up. No new evidence was discovered and no new suspects emerged. Time began to change people's stories as their memory lapsed through drugs and alcohol. Many of the calls they got were from the jail. There were inmates wanting to make a deal in pursuit of a shorter sentence. Stories poured in.

At the end of every year, the investigators would file a progress report. At the end of the annual report and every single interview came the disclaimer "There was no new evidence gathered by virtue of this report." As I poured over these reports for months, looking for clues, trying to understand what could be learned, my mind began to ask a question over and over: Why did they stop talking to Bobby Fort and anyone close to him? Bobby spent plenty of time drinking at the Labor Temple bar talking about Ada's murder. Much of his time there was spent with Rena Bambenek. Especially with Ada dead, how did interstate trafficking in firearms, buying and selling stolen property across state lines, just go away? How did Fort dodge the intense grilling of Ada's murder investigation that came out on Ed, Linda, Jack, and Jim? After 1985, I find no record of them ever bothering with Bobby Fort again, not by the Winona PD, FBI, BCA or the ATF. In the meantime, they questioned every rumor or jailhouse snitch who had a single word to say about Ada. Below is a sample of some of the interviews in the 1990's. The ones they did continue to work on the case, or seem to. I am not drawing a conclusion from these, other than they traveled all over the state to talk to people, file reports and make no arrest or find new evidence. Ada's murder remained unsolved in the 1990's.

BUREAU OF CRIMINAL APPREHENSION

Bureau number	Offense Category	MN offense code
85-388	Death investigation	9220

Count of Occurrence	Date and time of incident	Section
Winona	6-6-85	SPRO

Case title	Date and time of Activity
Ada Senenfelder	03-8-92

VICTIM
Senenfelder, Ada Francis- Previously identified

WITNESS
Bambenek, Rena Fay –DOB 7-24-55, Address 1761 7th street #C Winona

SYNOPSIS
On Friday, March 6, 1992 MNBCA special agents Gregory and MacLean conducted a second interview with Rena Bambenek at her residence in Winona

PERSONNEL ASSIGNED
MNBCA Special agents Richard Gregory and Kenneth MacLean

DETAILS

1. On Friday, March 6, 1992, at approximately 1000 hours, SA's Gregory and MacLean interviewed Rena Bambenek at her residence in Winona, Minnesota. Rena was baby-sitting during the interview and during the course of the interview, several persons came to the door and interrupted the interview with short conversations with Rena. SA Gregory informed Rena that the current investigation indicates that the information that Rena provided in the past to the investigations is now in question. SA Gregory informed Rena that the polygraph examination that Rena had taken in the past indicated that she may have withheld information at that time. Rena stated that she was then and is now afraid of the Bolstad family. Rena said that she wanted to cooperate now with the investigation and that she had liked Ada Senenfelder.

2. Rena told SA's Gregory and MacLean that she was aware of the problems between Ada Senenfelder and the Jim Bolstad family and Linda Erickson. Rena stated that she knew that Linda was angry at Ada because Ada's statements regarding alleged sexual conduct caused Jim Bolstad to be returned to jail. Rena stated that Linda Erickson and Jack Nissalke had taken Ada's radio and bicycle and had made several threats against Ada's safety. Rena told the SA's Gregory and MacLean that she knew that Erickson had threatened to kill Ada if Jim Bolstad did not get her out of Jail.

3. SA Gregory asked Rena why Rena was afraid of the Bolstad family. Rena stated that the Bolstad family would often times "hold court" with persons that the Bolstad family felt were stealing from our narcing on the activities of the Bolstad family. SA Gregory asked Rena if she was ever present when that happened. Rena states that she once saw the Bolstads hold court and that the offender was handcuffed to a chair and that Jack Nissalke beat him.

4. Rena told SA's Gregory and MacLean that on Wednesday, 6-6-85, that Linda and Ada were arguing again about Ada's statements to Jim Bolstad's parole officer, Mr. Hammes. Rena said that she heard Linda threaten to kill Ada on that occasion. Rena said that she was at Linda Erickson's apartment and was present when the threat was made. Rena said that Linda Erickson had just returned from seeing Jim Bolstad in jail and Ada had been at Erickson's apartment baby-sitting for Erickson's daughter Shannon Erickson. Rena said that she was there visiting with Ada and that Erickson told Ada "you do what we want or you're dead". Rena said that when she left, Ada was with Linda Erickson at Linda Erickson's apartment.

5. Rena told SA Gregory and MacLean that Linda Erickson wanted Ada to write a note to Mr. Hammes stating that Jim Bolstad was innocent of the allegations. Rena said that Ada refused to change her statement and Linda Erickson told Ada that she would be sorry.

6. SA MacLean asked Rena if Rena was at Ada's house on 6-5-85. Rena said that she drove Dennis Mickelson and Lori Bolstad over to Ada's house to pick up chicken with Ada had cooked. Rena stated that she drove to Ada's house, in the brown Mercury which belonged to James Bolstad. Rena said that she drove to Ada's house, and she remained in the car while Dennis Mickelson and Lori Bolstad went in and picked up the chicken from Ada. Rena said that she then drove Lori Bolstad and Dennis Mickelson back to Jim's apartment at Belview East. Rena said that she left Dennis Mickelson at the Belview East and that he took the chicken with him. Rena said that she then drove Lori Bolstad back to French Island in LaCrosse, Wisconsin. Rena said that after leaving Lori in Lacrosse, that she immediately returned to her apartment at Belview East in Winona.

7. Rena said that when she got back to her apartment, that Raymond Bolstad and Jack Nissalke immediately took the keys for the brown Mercury from Rena and that Raymond and Jack then drove away with the brown Mercury. Rena said that it appeared that Raymond and Jack had been waiting for her to return so they could leave with the Mercury. Rena stated that Ed Bolstad's vehicle, the gray Camaro, was not at the Belview East at that time. Rena said that she arrived home at about 2100 hours on 6-5-85 and was at her apartment for the remainder of the evening.

8. Rena told SA's Gregory and MacLean that she remained home because her daughter Allison, was sick. Rena stated that Dennis Mickelson came to the door during the evening of 6-5-85 and requested that Rena give him the keys to Jim Bolstad's apartment. Rena said that she did not have the keys to Bolstad's apartment. Rena described Mickelson at that time as dirty and sweating profusely as if he had been running. Rena said that Mickelson told her that he was going to "puke" and pass out at Bolstad's apartment. Rena said that she thought that it may have been around midnight when Mickelson came to her apartment.

9. SA Gregory asked Rena about a serious of telephone calls that she received and made sometime around midnight on 6-5-85. Rena said that she got a phone call from Linda Erickson and that Erickson invited Rena to come over to Erickson's for a party. Rena said that she told Erickson that it was late and that Allison was sick. Rena said that shortly have she talked with Erickson, she received a telephone call from Ed Bolstad. She said that Bolstad told her that he was at the Happy Chef restaurant and that Rena should call Linda Erickson and tell her to call him at the Happy Chef and that she should tell Erickson that the police will be coming to Linda's apartment. Rena said that she called Erickson and gave her Ed's message that he was at the Happy Chef and that the police would

be arriving at her apartment. Rena said that a short time later, she got another call from Ed. Rena said that Ed wanted to know if Rena had made the call to Linda, Rena told Ed that she had placed the call. Rena said that Ed then said that he was going to finish his coffee and go for a ride.

10. SA MacLean asked Rena if she saw Ed Bolstad on Thursday, 6-6-85, Rena said that Ed Bolstad came over to Rena's apartment for coffee sometime around 0800 hours on 6-6-85. Rena said that Bolstad was complaining about the traffic tickets he had gotten during the night. SA MacLean asked Rena to describe Ed Bolstad's appearance. Rena described Ed as being dirty and wearing brown corduroy pants and a plaid shirt. Rena said that she thought they were the same clothes that he was wearing the day before 6-6-85. Rena said that she saw Ray and Dennis remove two grocery bags from the Mercury and place the bags in the dumpster. Rena said that she also saw Ed Bolstad take a bag to the dumpster from Jim Bolstad's apartment.

11. Rena said that she saw Ray Bolstad, Danny Bolstad, Ed Bolstad, Dennis Mickelson, and Ty LNU (from LaCrosse) all get into the brown Mercury and leave Belview East. Rena estimated that the time they departed was sometime prior to 1030 hours.

12. SA MacLean asked Rena how she heard about Ada's death. Rena said that she was at her apartment doing chores when she heard on the radio that a woman had been found dead. Rena said that the woman's name was not given at the time but that she thought the address given was close to Ada's house. Rena said that she called Linda Erickson to see if Linda knew about it. Rena said that Erickson told Rena that she would pick Rena up and they would go together to Ada's to find out what was happening. Rena told SA MacLean and Gregory that about ten minutes after she

talked with Linda Erickson, Jack Nissalke called Rena and wanted to know if Rena heard about Ada being found dead. Rena that that Jack knew that it was Ada before that information had been made public. Rena said that Jack Nissalke then came over to Rena's apartment, picked up Rena and they went to Ada's. Rena said that Nissalke was driving Erickson's T-bird and that Erickson was not with Nissalke. Rena said that she felt that Nissalke had been at Linda Erickson's when Rena had called Erickson earlier. Rena said she left her daughter, Allison in the care of a neighbor, Steve Pagel.

13. Rena said that she and Nissalke drove to the crime scene at Ada's. Rena said the police spoke with Nissalke at the crime scene. Rena said that while they were in the crowd, that Dennis Mickelson walked over and joined her and Nissalke. Rena said that Nissalke wanted to wait and watch for Ada, "to be brought out in bags." Rena said that she wanted to leave.

14. Rena said that she and Mickelson drove to Donna Campbell's house. Rena said that Ed Bolstad was there working. Rena estimated that the time would have been sometime in the afternoon of 6-6-85, Rena said that Nissalke said that he had other business and told Mickelson to meet him at Belview East. Rena said that she had to get the T-bird back to Erickson because Erickson had to go to Lacrosse to see Jim Bolstad. Rena said that she drove to Erickson's and picked up Linda Erickson. Rena said that Erickson drove Rena back to Belview East and that Linda Erickson and Dennis Mickelson then drove to Lacrosse.

15. Rena told SA's Gregory and MacLean that she saw Ed Bolstad leaving Belview East with his parents, Julius and Adeline Bolstad sometime during the afternoon of 6-6-85.

16. Rena told SA's Gregory and MacLean that during the afternoon of 6-6-85 she received a phone call from Linda Erickson and Erickson told her that Jim Bolstad wanted Linda to have a party that night so that everyone could "get their story straight." Erickson told Rena to call Ed Bolstad and tell him about the meeting and call the Bolstad's and that she should also invite Julius and Adeline Bolstad. Rena said that she made the call to the Bolstads and that Thelma Nation (Bolstad) told her to please pick up Nickie Nation from the Bolstad's and bring Nickie to the nation's house when she was out picking up Ed.

17. Rena said that she picked up Ed and that she and Ed drove around until they went to Linda Erickson's apartment at about 2030 hours on 6-6-85.

18. SA Gregory asked Rena who was at the meeting /party at Erickson's apartment. Rena said that Linda Erickson, Ed Bolstad, Jack Nissalke, Dennis Mickelson, Raymond Bolstad, Danny Bolstad, Roger Bolstad, Lori Nissalke, and Rena were at the party. Rena said that Erickson said that Jim Bolstad wanted Danny and Raymond Bolstad back in the Lacrosse on the evening of 6-6-85. Rena said that Jack Nissalke was drunk during the party and that he threatened Rena. Dennis, Ed and Linda making knife cutting motions towards their respective throats and heads. Rena said that Erickson said that Ada got what she had coming to her. She should have signed that note Rena said that Linda Erickson told Rena to remember that if anyone asked that the brown Mercury did not leave Belview East at all night of 6-5-85 Rena said that Erickson told the group that Nissalke stayed at Erickson's apartment all night of 6-5-85 and that Mickelson stayed at Jim Bolstad's apartment on 6-5-85 and that Ed Bolstad had been at Julius Bolstad's farm during the night of 6-5-85.

19. SA MacLean asked Rena if Jack Nissalke and Linda Erickson were romantically involved during the time of Ada's murder. Rena told the agents that Nissalke and Erickson had a thing together during that time that Jim Bolstad was in jail. SA MacLean asked Rena to what degree Erickson and Jack were involved, Rena told SA Gregory and MacLean that she saw Nissalke and Erickson in bed together at Jim Bolstad's apartment before the time Ada had died. Rena told SA Gregory MacLean that she knew that Erickson bought clothes and other presents for Jack Nissalke during that time. SA MacLean asked Rena if June Bolstad and Jack Nissalke also intimate with June Bolstad and that both Linda Erickson and June Bolstad knew about the others involvement with Nissalke. The interview was concluded at approximately 1300 hours on 3-6-92.

STATUS AND APPRAISAL OF INVESTIGATION
Investigation continues.

Bureau of Criminal Apprehension

Bureau Number	Offense Category	MN offense code
85000388	Death Investigation	9220

County of occurrence	Date and time	Submitted by
Winona	06-06-85	SA Richard Gregory

Case title
ADA Senenfelder Death Investigation

VICTIM
   1. Senenfelder, Ada Frances – previously identified

WITNESS
Pagel, Steven C – Dob 12/25/58, address 477 East Sixth street, Winona, Minnesota

SYNOPSIS
In the morning of April 10, 1992 MN BCA special agents Gregory and MacLean interviewed Steve Pagel at his residence in Winona, Minnesota to obtain background information concerning his association with the Bolstad family and to obtain information concerning activities at his residence on the night of June 5, 1985

DETAILS
1. Steven Pagel said that in the summer of 1985 he was living in an apartment with Vicky Wicka which was located next to Ed Bolstad's apartment on Belleview Street in Winona, Minnesota. Pagel explained that he partied with the Bolstad family and because they lived next door to Wicka, he had become acquainted with Wicka. Pagel said that he then moved in with Wicka and discontinued his partying with Bolstad because Wicka did not drink.

2. Pagel was then asked to provide information concerning the activities at his apartment of the evening of June 5, 1985. Pagel said that he and Vicky Wicka were upstairs in their apartment between 11 p.m. and 11:30 p.m.
On June 5, 1985 he heard a car door slam. Pagel said that upon hearing the car door slam he looked out the window and saw Ed Bolstad getting out of his tan, or brown automobile.

3. Pagel said that he noticed Bolstad was carrying a shirt in his and that he was not wearing a shirt.

4. Pagel then stated that he went outside and talked briefly with Ed Bolstad, Pagel advised he could not remember what clothing Bolstad was wearing at the time, however he remembered that Bolstad was very sweaty, that the ends of his hair were wet from what appeared to be perspiration and that he did not have a shirt on and was carrying a shirt wadded up in his hand. Pagel said that Bolstad commented that he had been drinking with Linda and the group and come home to get a shirt because he had gotten his shirt wet.

5. When asked why Pagel went out and talked with Ed Bolstad, Pagel first commented that he and Bolstad were friends and he just went out to talk with him because of that reason. Later in the interview, Pagel was reminded that possibly he and Vicky Wicka had the key to the Ed Bolstad's apartment and Pagel stated that he thought possibly that's why he went out to talk with Ed Bolstad was because he knew he had Bolstad's key.

6. Pagel said that he did not notice any blood on Ed Bolstad on that evening and did not remember seeing anyone other than Bolstad come to the Bolstad apartment that evening. Pagel said he did not remember seeing Dennis Mickelson that evening. Pagel also said that he may or may not have gotten cigarettes from Rena Bambenek because getting cigarettes from her was somewhat of an everyday occurrence.

7. Pagel did not state that he noticed there was blood on the walls however he was never present when the Bolstads "held court" and did not see anyone else go in Bolstad's apartment on that evening.

8. Pagel said that he believed Ed Bolstad may have been in the Bolstad apartment for approximately 15 minutes on that evening, however, because Pagel went inside of his apartment he did not actually see Bolstad leave. Pagel said that he did not see anyone else go in Bolstads apartment on that evening.

9. Pagel said he could not remember what he did the next day, and the next thing he remembered is the police being at the apartment with a van, going through Ed's apartment. Pagel said that Vicky Wicka told him that Ada Senenfelder was dead and he believed this conversation took place while the police were at the Bellview apartments searching Ed's apartment.

10. Pagel said he had never been to Linda Erickson's apartment and had never been to Ada Senenfelder's apartment and had only partied with the Bolstads at Ed Bolstad's apartment or at Prairie Island.

11. Pagel said that he remembered Ed Bolstads brown car was parked in front of Rena's apartment on that evening.

12. Pagel said that he did not see Jack Nissalke on that evening.

13. Pagel said that Rena Bambenek seemed quite nervous after the killing of Senenfelder and seemed to be hiding something.

14. Pagel said that he had not seen or talked with the Bolstads since about a week after the Ada Senenfelder homicide.

Pagel said that he never did see Ed Bolstad return to the Bolstad apartment after the evening of June 5, 1985.

15. End of the interview

BUREAU OF CRIMINAL APPREHENSION

Bureau number	Offense Category	MN offense code
85000388	Death investigation	9220

Count of Occurrence	Date and time of incident	Section
Winona	6-6-85	SPRO

Case title	Date and time of Activity
Ada Senenfelder	4-20-92

VICTIM
Senenfelder, Ada Francis- Previously identified

WITNESS
Dennis John Mickelson, dob 9/17/65 current address 400 Monitor Street, Apartment 14 Lacrosse, Wisconsin

SYNOPSIS
On Friday, April 10th 1992 at approximately 1642 hours, SA Gregory and MacLean interviewed Dennis Mickelson at his residence in the LaCrosse, Wisconsin. Mickelson is currently living with Brenda Howe. Howe and Mickelson were both in attendance at the party at Linda Erickson's apartment on June 5, 1985, in Winona, Minnesota.

PERSONNEL ASSIGNED
Mn BCA Special Agents Gregory and MacLean

DETAILS

1. On Friday, April 10, 1992 at approximately 1642 hours, Dennis Mickelson arrived at his residence at 400 Monitor Street, Lacrosse Wisconsin. He was accompanied by an unidentified male. MN BCA special agents Gregory and MacLean were in the process of concluding the interview with Brenda Howe when Mickelson arrived home. Prior to arriving at home, Mickelson went into the bedroom of the apartment and remained there throughout the interview with Mickelson and Howe.

2. Mickelson claimed not to remember details of the events surrounding June 5 and 6, 1985. Mickelson admitted to agents that he had smoked marijuana just prior to the interview with the agents. Mickelson said that he smokes marijuana to relax. The agents informed Mickelson that he had given conflicting information when he was interviewed in June 1985. Mickelson said that he did not recall that he had given conflicting stories but said that he had been "intimidated by all cops asking questions". Mickelson told the agents that he had nothing to now hide and that he would tell the truth. Mickelson said that he was afraid of the Bolstad family in 1985 and that they were "goofy" and that "they could pull a gun out and shoot you."

3. Mickelson said that he never lived with Ada Senenfelder. The agents pointed out that Mickelson said that he had lived with Ada Senenfelder. Mickelson said that he only used Ada's house and address as a mailing address so that he could receive food stamps. Mickelson said that Ed Bolstad had explained to Mickelson how to be eligible to

get food stamps and suggested that Mickelson use Ada's address. Mickelson said that he never had a key to Ada's house. Mickelson denied that he left his clothes at Ada's but Mickelson did say that he may have left a jacket or other minor clothing items at Ada's.

4. Mickelson said it "seems like I remember being at Linda's when the police came." Mickelson also said that "I had to have been there until 11:00PM or midnight." The police reports indicate that the police were at the party at 0043 hours on June 6, 1985. Mickelson said that he left the party by himself and that he left by the back door of Erickson's apartment. Mickelson said that he remembers that steps were made of iron. Mickelson said that he remembers that he walked back to the Bolstad apartment at 755 Bellview and that he crossed the bridge near the Lake.

5. Mickelson said that he walked back to Ed/Jim Bolstad's apartment at 755 Bellview. Mickelson said that he went next door to the Bolstad's apartment, to the apartment of Vicky Wicka and asked her boyfriend, Steve Pagel, for the key to the Bolstad's apartment. Mickelson said that Pagel was supposed to have had the key because Pagel and Wicka were doing their laundry at the Bolstad apartment. Mickelson said that Pagel did not have the key to the Bolstad's and Pagel suggested to Mickelson that Mickelson climb in the window, since the window was usually open. Mickelson said that he crawled into the Bolstad's apartment and that he went up to his and Raymond Bolstad's room and "crashed." Mickelson said that when he woke up the following morning, everyone was freaked out about the turtle we had cut the head off, or somebody cut the head off of the turtle, at the park. Mickelson said that there was

blood all over the backseat of Ed Bolstad's car. Mickelson said that it was Danny Bolstad's idea to clean out Ed Bolstad's car that day. Mickelson said that they put whatever they took out of the car in a bag and placed the bag in the dumpster. Mickelson said that the police told him that they had everything that had been in the dumpster.

6. Mickelson said that everyone was freaking out after hearing about Ada. Mickelson said that he was worried because he knew her and he thought that everyone was going to be questioned, and that he had been "fucked up" and by himself. Consequently, he would not have had an alibi. Mickelson said that they drove to Ada's and saw the yellow strings and they then returned to 755 Bellview.

7. Mickelson informed the agents that he could not remember going to Ada Senenfelder's with Laurie Bolstad on June 5, 1985. Mickelson said that he did not remember going over to Ada's to get chicken. Mickelson said that he thought that he remembered that the group was supposed to go to Ada's for ham dinner on the evening of June 5, at about 8 or 8:30 p.m. Mickelson said that he thought the reason the group didn't go to Ada's was because everyone was getting too drunk to go while they were at the Ericksons' party.

8. Mickelson said that he knows no one in the group that would have killed Ada, because they all knew her. Mickelson said that maybe it was Ada's husband or boyfriend or someone that Ada had caused to go to jail. Mickelson that he thought that Jim Bolstad was in jail for raping Ada's daughter or something. Mickelson said that Ada was always hitting on Ed and that Rena Bambenek

really liked Ed Bolstad. Mickelson said that Rena was the only one that was ever "pissed" at Ada.

9. Mickelson said that he doesn't remember that he went with Danny Bolstad to the Winona when Danny Bolstad went to recant his original interview. Danny Bolstad originally drew a picture of the blood spots on the clothes that he said he removed from Ed's car on the morning of June 6, 1985. Mickelson said that maybe the reason that they went to change their story was because maybe Danny had been told to do so. The agents asked Mickelson if anyone told him what to say when the police questioned him. Mickelson said that he was told not to say anything about the ham at Ada's and to say that he stayed at the party at Linda Erickson's all night of June 5, 1985. Mickelson did not say who told him what to tell the police if questioned.

BUREAU OF CRIMINAL APPREHENSION

Bureau number	Offense Category	MN offense code
85000388	Death investigation	9220

Count of Occurrence	Date and time of incident	Section
Winona	6-6-85	SPRO

Case title	Date and time of Activity
Ada Senenfelder	10-16-95

VICTIM
Senenfelder, Ada Francis—Previously identified

WITNESS
Mathot, Helen Jo 1759 5th Street, Winona, Minn.

SYNOPSIS
This is a summary of a taped statement taken from Ms. Mathot concerning the Senenfelder case.

PERSONNEL ASSIGNED
SA Hern Dybevik and Winona police Det. Al Muelen

DETAILS
1. On 10/16/95 at approximately 1338 hours Ms. Mathot came to Winona police department and met with and interviewed with investigators in this case. Investigator Mueller called Ms. Mathot earlier in the day and asked her to come to the police department in regards to some questions that the investigators had about this investigation.

2. Ms. Mathot is the mother of Jennifer Barness.

3. Ms. Mathot had previously provided information to investigator Mueller concerning the Senenfelder investigation.

4. Mathot said that on the night of the Senenfelder murder she took her daughter, Jennifer Barness to the intersection of 3rd and Walnut in Winona. This is approximately five to eight blocks away from the Senenfelder residence. Mathot stated later in the evening before sunrise she received a call from her daughter and wanted to be picked up at the same address. Mathot said that she did go to that address and picked up her daughter. Mathot said when the call came from her daughter to come pick her up that her daughter was frantic on the phone she said. Mathot stated that when she got to 3rd and Walnut, Jennifer got in her car and said "get me out of here. I can't talk," Mathot said that at that time she knew something very bad had happened, but her daughter wasn't telling her everything.

5. Mathot stated that the next day she heard the news about Ada's death. She realized her daughter had been talking about it. She also stated that she remembers her daughter saying there is blood all over. She mentioned murder and she also mentioned the name Bolstad in her conversations.

CITY OF WINONA POLICE DEPARTMENT
SUPPLEMENTAL REPORT

October 17, 1995

Subject: Interview of Helen Mathot

Personal Assigned: Inv Al. Mueller
                    City of Winona Police Department

                    S/A Herm Dybevik

Synopsis:

On 10/16/95, above officers interviewed Helen Mathot at
LEC in Winona MN. During the interview she related
conversations which she had with her daughter Jennifer
Sorum, Aka Barness. Those conversations indicated that
Jennifer had direct or 2nd hand information about the
murder of Ada Senenfelder.

Details:

On about 3/21/94, writer received a call from Helen
Mathot. Helen related that her daughter Jennifer, aka
Jennifer Barness, had possibly been involved in the murder
of Ada Senenfelder. She stated that her daughter was
pregnant and was expecting on 4/24/94. She called writer
on this particular date because her daughter was frantic,
very scared and unstable because of Roger Bolstad and
McNamer had just visited her daughter. She felt it had to
do with the Senenfelder homicide as her daughter told her
she knew of or was involved in that murder.

Writer knew that Roger Bolstad had been living in Kellogg,
Minnesota, but did not recall a police report dated

3/20/94, ICR#94002985, which indicated that Roger Bolstad and a David McNamer had been in Winona on 3-20-94 giving me some credibility to the report of Jennifer. Helen then released the following information.

- That Jennifer told her that she knew of or was involved in the murder of Ada Senenfelder.
- That Jennifer told Helen that if Jennifer were killed, Jennifer wanted Helen to know where to start looking.
- That Jennifer told her that Roger Bolstad held the woman down and Albert Bolstad stabbed the woman.
- That other people present were Jeannie Wicka, Richard Murphy, Mary Zimmerman, Eva LNU, Barry Ring
- That Jennifer married Jeff Barness to protect Jennifer from the Bolstads
- That Jennifer is Jennifer Sorum who currently resided at 109 Jefferson Street in Houston, MN with an unlisted phone number.
- That Albert Bolstad had been living with Eva across from the monastery near Stockton, MN.
- That Jennifer was going with Barry Ring at the time of the murder, Barry lived with a Dionysius in a house kitty corner from the Town and Country bank in Winona.
- Jennifer was pregnant by Barry Ring but miscarried.
- About two weeks before the murder, Albert cut off some of Eva's fingers at the first joint and Jennifer had witnessed it.
- That as Jennifer and Barry had left the party, They could hear Ada screaming and knew that Roger held her down and Albert stabbed her.
- That Eva is Eva Savoy.
- That Jennifer lives in a gold house next to a farm implement dealer in Houston.

- That Lorraine, Richard Murphy's ex-wife, lives in a green house across the street from Jennifer.

At about 1330 on 10/16/95, S/A Dybevik and writer interviewed Helen Mathot in an interview room in the police department. Officers had previously interviewed her daughter Jennifer and wanted to get a formal interview with Helen. The interview was recorded by S/A Dybevik.

Helen reaffirmed the information that she had previously given writer which was listed above.

Helen also recalled that on the night of the murder, Jennifer had asked Helen for a ride downtown and Helen recalled dropping Jennifer off in the area of 3rd and Walnut Street. Helen stated she got a call in the middle of the night from Jennifer who was frantic and needed a ride right away. Helen then went and picked Jennifer up in the same place she had dropped her off. Jennifer told her to get away from there as there was a murder, Bolstads were mentioned and Jennifer commented about blood being all over. Helen later recalled that she picked up Jennifer up between 2 a.m. and 4 a. m. that night.

Helen found out about the murder of Ada the following morning and realized that Jennifer may have been involved. Over the next couple of days she tried to get more information from Jennifer.

Jennifer related that she heard screaming and ran. Helen also related that she had called the police at the time to relate what she knew about her daughter but that her daughter was never interviewed.

Disposition:
Additional follow – up investigation to follow.

CITY OF WINONA POLICE DEPARTMENT
OCTOBER 27, 1995
SUPPLEMENTAL REPORT

OCA# 85631
Offense: Homicide
Complainant: Ada Senenfelder
By: Inv. Al Mueller

Subject: Interview with unknown male

Personnel assigned.
        Inv. Al Mueller
        Asst. Chief Jerrie Seibert
        City of Winona Police Department

Synopsis:
On 10/24/95, officers met with an unidentified male at a bridge construction site in Winona County. This male related to officers that his girlfriend Jennifer Barness, had recently talked with her regarding the murder of Ada. She told this male details of the murder but he could not recall all of them as he was somewhat drunk at the time. The male stated that he would be willing to wear a recorder and go back in and try to get her to talk about it again.

Details: At about 1200 on 10/24/1995, Chief Seibert and writer went to a location in Winona County to meet with an unknown male that purported to have information regarding the Ada Senenfelder murder. The directions are on the attached report of Winona County Dispatcher Ev. Holz.

On arrival officers noted a 3 man crew working on a newly completed bridge on Winona County Highway 25. Officers waited for a while and then were waved over to a van by one of the workers when they took a break. The van, which appeared to belong to the male that waved us over MN registration 19LTS. A Construction equipment trailer parked nearby had the name "Lunda Construction, Black River Falls Wisc." painted on the side. Writer drove the unmarked squad car over to the van and the male got in the backseat. Officers introduced themselves to the male who would not identify himself to the officers at this point. He explained that he has been seeing a "Jenny" who the police recently talked to regarding the Ada Senenfelder murder. He stated the following.

• That Jenny recently told him that the police talked to her recently about the Senenfelder murders.
• That she related part of the story of then murder to him.
• That he was intoxicated at the time and does not recall all of the details of the story she told.
• That he did recall that she told him that a kid named Sanders held her Ada's legs at the time of the murder.
• That Jenny is afraid that the Bolstads will cut her throat if she cooperates.
• That Sanders told her about the murder.
• That male stated that he would be willing to cooperate further and would be willing to wear a tape recorder to go in and talk with her about the murder.

He explained that he met Jenny about 6 months ago and sees her several times a week. Writer advised him that we might do such an interview and asked how writer could get in touch with him. He stated call Richard or Mary and ask them or leave a message that Al called. Writer gave him a business card with writer's phone number for the return call. Writer advised him that writer would contact him in the following week. The interview ended and a recording of the interview was secured with other interview tapes in a locked file in Writer's office.

CITY OF WINONA POLICE DEPARTMENT
OCTOBER 27, 1995
SUPPLEMENTAL REPORT

OCA# 85631
Offense: Homicide
Complainant: Ada Senenfelder
By: Inv. Al Mueller

Subject:
Interview with James Oliver Moody

Personnel assigned.
>   Inv. Al Mueller
>   City of Winona Police Department

Details
On 10-27-95, writer interviewed James Oliver Moody,
DOB 5-6-38 in the jail at the LEC. During the interview,
Jim seemed to recall some details about the night after the
murder while not recalling others. He stuck to the story he
gave in his interview dated 6/13/1985 and could not recall
making any threats as related in a waitress interviewed by
Dave Knight dated 7/3/1985.

Disposition
At about 1326 on 10/27/95, writer went to the Winona
county LEC jail to interview James Moody. The interview
took place in the interview room that is located hear the
north door of the jail.

On entering, writer introduced himself to Mr. Moody
Because Mr. Moody was incarcerated on an unrelated

matter, writer read him the Winona County Notification Of Rights form. He refused to sign it stating that his attorney that had just been appointed on the other charge, had advised him not to sign anything. I asked if he understood the rights I had read and he stated that he did. He identified himself as James Oliver Moody. He stated that when he gets out of jail he will be moving to Wabash County. Currently he lives at the Acorn apartments #5. Prior to the notification of rights, writer did advise him that writer wanted to talk with him about the murder of Ada Senenfelder.

During questioning, Moody kept to his story about going to into the Country Kitchen on 6-7-85 for the purpose of meeting with Jamie Dixon. When asked why he later threatened a waitress for talking with the police regarding this matter he stated that this was the first he heard of it. He denied doing it and could not recall doing it.

He did recall vividly, that on the morning of 6/7/85, he was with his "girl" and that he yelled at Jamie Dixon who was in a yellow cab, to meet him at the Country Kitchen. That is why he asked for Dixon. He denied looking for or asking about the Bolstads that morning.

He also stated that he had seen the Bolstad's in the Country Kitchen several weeks before that and may have talked to them but did not see them again for a long time. He stated that he had known the Bolstad's before as he kind of grew up with them and their families knew each other.

He stated that on the day the body was discovered he was painting his Aunt's house which was about ½ block from the murder scene and he recalled walking down to see what was going on.

Moody could think of no reason anyone would lie about his activities at the Country Kitchen around the time of the murder. Writer explained that it appeared that he may be involved in the murder or at least involved in tampering with a witness in a murder case based on the reports that we had that were in conflict with his statements. Writer advised him to think about it some more and get back in touch with writer if he wanted to change his statement before the case goes to trial. The interview was recorded but the tape ran out near the end of the interview, it will be secured with the other interview tapes.

BUREAU OF CRIMINAL APPREHENSION

Bureau number	Offense Category	MN offense code
85000388	Death investigation	9220

Count of Occurrence	Date and time of incident	Section
Winona	6-6-85	SPRO

Case title	Date and time of Activity
Ada Senenfelder	11-9-95

Victim
Senenfelder Ada Francis as previously described

Witness
Murphy, Laureen Marie, DOB 6-1-56, 313 West Maple Houston, TX

Synopsis
This is a summary of a taped statement taken from Laureen Murphy at Houston police department.

Personnel Assigned
SA Herm Dybevik and Winona Police Det. Al Mueller

Details.
    1. On 11-9-95, at approximately 1425 hours, investigators Dybevik and Mueller met Ms. Murphy at the Houston Police department offices in downtown Houston. The purpose of the interview was to interview Ms. Murphy as to her knowledge of what went on during the period of the Senenfelder murder in Winona Minnesota

about the murder of Ada Senenfelder. She stated that she never knew who Ada was she had only heard of the murder but with no details.

2. She stated that in 1980 she married a person by the name of Dick Murphy. They were married in Decorah, Iowa. In 1981 she divorced Dick in Houston County. From 1981 until 1986 Murphy and her ex-husband were separated however occasionally would get back together. In 1986 Murphy and her ex-husband moved back in with each other and tried to reconcile their marriage. This took place on Onalaska, Wisconsin and this lasted for approximately 3 months. After the three months of living with each other again, Murphy decided that she had enough of Dick Murphy's abuse and once and for all moved out.

3. Murphy stated that during 1986 while she was living with Dick in Onalaska Wisconsin she remembered several of the Bolstad's and some other people were involved in the planning of an armed robbery in Winona, Minn. She stated that she was not part of that place the planning was done at their residence at Onalaska Wisconsin. And she stated that her former husband Dick Murphy was involved with that. Up to this time she had not heard of Ada nor knew of Senenfelder's murder.

4. Her ex-husband associated quite often with the Bolstad's and several of their friends she stated that she knew who these people were did not especially care for them and did not associate with them.

5. Murphy stated that after living with Dick Murphy she eventually ended up in Houston County, Minn., where she

met up with a friend of hers by the name of Kevin Johnson. While living in Houston County and the city of Houston, she eventually got to know and became good friends with Jennifer Barness. Murphy stated that in 1992, She met Jennifer Barness for the first time. During this conversation they started asking each other about difference acquaintances that they had when each of them lived in Winona. This is the first time Murphy was told about the Ada Senenfelder's murder in detail. If it were not for Jennifer sharing she would not have the details she did today.

6. She stated that her ex-husband's full name is Dickie Dean Murphy and his DOB is 8-2-51. He is currently living in Perry, GA and has lived there for the past five to seven years

7. Just prior to the end of the interview, Murphy stated that it's a funny thing that the investigators were talking with her today about the murder and about Jennifer Barness because she stated that approximately two hours before meeting with the investigators that Jennifer called her home today and talked with her. Murphy stated that Jennifer Barness seemed very happy and just wanted to talk and renew their friendship. Barness told her that she was currently working at the Holiday Inn in Winona. Barness did not mention or talk about the Senenfelder murder at all.

8. Murphy stated that after thinking about some of the questions that were asked today of her, She would go back home and think on it and if anything came to mind as far as details she would either give the detective a call.

Description of custody of evidence:

There is one microcassette tape take from this interview and it will become part of the Winona police department.

BUREAU OF CRIMINAL APPREHENSION
Report of Investigation

Annual Update

85000388 Homicide   SA Herm E. Dybevik

Winona   6-3-85
ADA FRANCIS SENENFELDER

Victim
Senenfelder, Ada Francis, as previously described

Synopsis
This is an annual Case review

Personnel Assigned
SA Herm Dybevik

Details
1. SA Dybevik continues to be in contact with Winona Police detective Al Mueller in reference to this homicide investigation. During 1995, Inv. Mueller and SA Dybevik met on a couple of different occasions and discussed the future of this investigation.

2. There were three interviews conducted during 1995 in regards to this investigation. The first interview was done on 10-16-95 at approximately 1140 hours, and the person interviewed at this particular time was Jennifer Lee Barness. A taped statement was taken of that interview, and an investigation report was also made.

John K. Bucher   129

3. The second interview that was done was on 10-16-1995 at 1338 hours. The person interviewed was Helen Jo Mathot. There was a taped statement taken of that interview, as well as an investigation report was filed in reference to that interview.

4. The third interview during 1995 on this investigation was taken from Laureen Marie Murphy. There was also a taped statement taken of this interview, as well as an investigation report filed.

5. On 1/2/96, SA Dybevik and Doolittle went to the Winona police department and met with Inv. Al Mueller of the Winona police department. The purpose of the interview was for the three investigators to review this case and possibly make the initial plans for doing a Task force in conjunction with the cold case unit of Minnesota Bureau of Criminal Apprehension.

6. SA Doolittle briefed Inv. Mueller on the cold case unit and what items the cold case unit could offer. SA Doolittle also stated that before pursuing anything in reference to this case,that he would like to talk with the county attorney in reference to a few issues in this matter before proceeding with any type of Task Force or any type of involvement with the cold case unit. SA Dybevik and Doolittle attempted to contact the Winona county attorney on that particular day, and no contact was made. SA Doolittle stated that he would be in contact with the Winona county attorney and discuss these issues and would be getting back to SA Dybevik and Inv. Mueller at a later date.

7. SA Dybevik and Inv. Mueller discussed this case after meeting with SA Doolittle, and it was determined that, if at all possible, the Mueller would appreciate having the cold case unit involved in this investigation, but he and his department is not ready to pursue this major of an investigation at this particular time. Inv. Mueller thought that maybe later in 1996 would be a more appropriate time. to take on such a venture with this investigation

DESCRIPTION AND CUSTODY OF EVIDENCE
There was no evidence gathered by virtue of this report.

BUREAU OF CRIMINAL APPREHENSION

Bureau number   Offense Category   MN offense code
85000388   Death investigation   9220

Count of Occurrence   Date and time of incident Section
Winona   6-6-85   SPRO

Case title   Date and time of Activity
Ada Senenfelder   1-30-1997

Victim
Senenfelder, Ada Francis – Previously identified

Synopsis
This is an annual case update

Personnel Assigned
SA Herm Dybevik

Details
1. It was the intention of SA Dybevik and investigator Al Mueller of the Winona Police department, to continue to follow-up on this investigation during 1996.

2. The County Attorney for Winona County became very ill during the 1996 and was unable to proceed with this investigation. The county attorney passed away during the latter part of 1996

3. It was agreed upon by investigator Mueller and SA Dybevik that proceeding with this investigation would be

put on hold until a new county attorney for Winona County would be hired. It was also decided that the investigators would then approach a new county attorney and make an attempt to explain the investigation to that person at that time.

4. S/A Dybevik had spoken briefly with the new county attorney, Chuck MacLean. It was decided between S/A Dybevik and Mr. MacLean that sometime in the early part of 1997, Mr. MacLean would get together with the investigators and agencies involved in this investigation and began a review of the case.

5. There was no further investigations or interviews done on this case during 1996.

Description and custody Evidence
No evidence gathered by virtue of this report.

CITY OF WINONA POLICE DEPARTMENT
SUPPLEMENTAL REPORT

CFS# 85631   Date June 18, 1992
Offense: Homicide
Complainant: Ada Senenfelder
Report by: Inv. Al Mueller

On 6-17-1992 at about 1115 writer interviewed Ted Larson. Ted is a recently retired deputy from the Winona county Sheriff's Office.

Earlier on 6/17/92 Ted transported Albert Bolstad to the Zumbro Valley Facility, Albert was very intoxicated and was sent to Zumbro Valley after a domestic in which he beat up his dad.

During the trip Albert talked about the Ada case. He stated that Ken went into the Navy when it happened. He also said that Ken is getting out of the service this month. Albert also stated that Ken lived a couple of blocks from the Mankato bar.

Albert stated that Ken had bragged about doing this thing with Ada. Albert said that it was stupid for Ken to have done that. Albert repeated that several times during the trip. Ted stated that Albert was drunk when he made the statements and mistook Ted for Sheriff Spitzer.

Albert tested at .36 BAC.

CITY OF WINONA POLICE DEPARTMENT
SUPPLEMENTAL REPORT

July 9, 1996

CASE # 85631
Offense: Homicide
Complainant: Ada Senenfelder
Report by: Inv. Al Mueller

Subject: Interview of Dennis Henry

Personnel Assigned: Inv. Al Mueller
                City Of Winona Police Department

Details:

On 7-8-96 at about 1630, writer called Dennis Henry at
507-894-8021. Writer had previously received a note from La
Crosse County regarding Mr. Henry having some information
about a murder weapon involved in the Senenfelder homicide (See
attached note).

Mr. Henry explained to writer that he had been married to a Kelly
Clinkscales for about 13 years. He is currently divorced from her
and has custody of their children. He stated that she is in some sort
of intensive treatment in Onalaska Wisconsin but that he is still
having domestic problems with her.

Mr. Henry also stated that several years ago he did talk to law
enforcement about this same information.

Mr. Henry stated that between 1986 and 1988 Kelly had been out
on a drinking binge. He stated that at that time she showed him
some sort of hunting knife. She told him that it had been involved

in something in Winona. He stated that she did not state who gave it to her and no names were mentioned. Only that it was possibly involved in an unsolved homicide. He described that knife as being a plain hunting knife without a sheath. Kelly later claimed she took the knife to her brother's house and left it there.

Mr. Henry does not think Kelly will be cooperative with law enforcement at this time. She is fighting to get custody of her kids back.

He stated that he would be willing to cooperate however as he knows Kelly's brother in the cities and gets along with him. He stated that we would talk to her brother in the near future and then let writer know what he finds out about the knife.

BUREAU OF CRIMINAL APPREHENSION

Bureau number   Offense Category   MN offense code
85000388   Death investigation   9220

Count of Occurrence   Date and time of incident   Section
Winona   6-6-85   SPRO

Case title   Date and time of Activity
Ada Senenfelder   2-14-92

Victim
Ada Senenfelder- previously identified

Subjects
Bolstad, Edward J- DOB 3-17-52 Address 755 Belview, Apartment
E, Winona, Minnesota

Erickson,Linda DOB 12-31-61 Address 914 Parks Street
Apartment 221, Winona Minnesota

Synopsis
The purpose of this report is to document the driving time and
distance between the victim's residence, 566 East Fourth Street,
and Erickson's residence, 914 Parks Street, and Bolstad's residence,
755 Belleview.

Personnel Assigned
MN BCA special agents Richard Gregory and Ken MacLean.

Details
1. On the afternoon of February 14, 1992 SAs MacLean and
Gregory drove from the victim's residence on East Fourth

street to the apartments of Linda Erickson and Ed Bolstad for the purpose of determining the driving time and the distance to the various locations. The times represented driving these distances during mid-afternoon and at normal driving speed. Also the distance and time would reflect the most direct route between the locations. The driving time and distances were noted as follows:

From	To	Distance	Time
566 east 4th st.	755 Bellview	1.0 mile	2.5 m
755 Bellview	914 Parks Ave	.8 mile	2.15 s
566 East 4th	914 Parks Ave	1.8 mile	4.45s
755 Bellview	Happy Chef	3.0 mile	7m 8s

BUREAU OF CRIMINAL APPREHENSION

Bureau number	Offense Category	MN offense code
85000388	Death investigation	9220

Count of Occurrence	Date and time of incident	Section
Winona	6-6-85	SPRO

Case title	Date and time of Activity
Ada Senenfelder	3-3-1992

Subject
Senenfelder, ADA

Witness
Rena Fay Bambenek- DOB 7-13-55 1761 West 7th Street Apartment C, Winona, Minnesota

Synopsis
On February 26, 1992, MN BCA special agents Gregory and MacLean interviewed Rena Bambenek at her residence at 1761 West 7th Street Apartment C, Winona Minnesota. Bambenek was a friend and neighbor of Jim Bolstad at the time of Ada Senenfelder's death.

Personnel Assigned
MN BCA Special Agents Gregory and MacLean

Details
1. On February 26, 1992 at approximately 1500 hours, special agents Gregory and MacLean interviewed Rena Bambenek at her residence at 1761 West 7th Street, apartment C, Winona, Minnesota. Present during various

segments of the interview were two unidentified white males and one black male. The presence of the unidentified males may have inhibited the interview. Also present during the interview was Bambenek's child, Allison Bambenek.

2 . Rena Bambenek said that on the evening of June 5, 1985, the night of the party at Linda Erickson's apartment, that Rena Bambenek drove Laurie Bolstad and Dennis Mickelson to Ada Senenfelder's house to pick up ham because Ed Bolstad asked Rena to do this. Rena said that she did not go into Ada's house but rather she remained in the car while Laurie Bolstad and Dennis Mickelson went into Ada's house. Rena stated that she drove Ed Bolstad's brown Mercury car and that she though she may have used the headlights while en route to Ada's house. Rena said that Mickelson brought chicken from Ada's house and not ham. Rena said that she dropped Dennis Mickelson back at Jim Bolstad's apartment. Rena said that when Laurie Bolstad returned to the car Laurie said, Ada would call the boys to come and get the ham. Rena said that after she dropped Dennis Mickelson at Jim Bolstad's apartment that she drove Laurie Bolstad to La Crosse, Wisconsin.

3 . Rena stated that she then drove to La Crosse with Laurie Bolstad and then immediately returned to her apartment in Winona. Rena said when she brought Ed Bolstad's Mercury back to Jim Bolstad's apartment in Winona. That Ray Bolstad and Jack Nissalke immediately took the keys for the car and drove away with the Mercury. Rena said that the next time she saw Ed Bolstad's Mercury was on the morning of June 6, 1985, and it was parked in front of Jim Bolstad's apartment and that Raymond Bolstad, the son of Jim Bolstad, was cleaning the car out. It should be noted

that Rena Bambenek lived in the apartment B and Jim lived in apartment E. Rena said that she only had the ignition and truck key for Ed Bolstad's Mercury and that she did not have any other keys for the Bolstad's apartment or other cars. Rena stated that she gave the keys to Raymond Bolstad. Rena was unable to say what time she returned to Winona however she said that she arrived back in Winona using headlights for driving.

The case file indicates that sunset on June 5, 1985 was at 2045 hours.

4. Rena sated that she did not go to Linda Erickson's at Northwood apartments on the evening Of June 5, 1985. Rena stated that she remained at home because her daughter, Allison had a cold. Rena stated that she remembered that Dennis Mickelson knocked at the door sometime during the evening and asked for the keys to Jim Bolstad's apartment. Rena told Mickelson that she did not have the keys and Mickelson then crawled through the broken window into Jim Bolstad's apartment. Rena said that Mickelson appeared to have been sweating as though he had been running. Rena said that Mickelson told her that he was going to pass out. Rena said that she did not remember talking to Steve Pagel, her neighbor, during the evening of June 5, 1985 Rena said that it was her impression that Pagel had been to the party and Linda Erickson's during the evening of June 5, 1985.

5. Rena said that Linda Erickson called Rena during the evening of June 5, 1985, to invite Rena to her party. Rena said that she declined because her daughter was in bed with a cold. Rena said that her daughter, Allison, is typically in

bed by 2100 hours. Rena said that Linda wanted to know if Jack Nissalke was there with Rena. Rena told the special agents that Jack was not with her.

Rena said that shortly after Linda initially called Rena, that Ed Bolstad called Rena and told Rena that if Linda Erickson calls, Rena should tell Linda, "I am at the Happy Chef." SA MacLean asked Rena why she thought that Ed Bolstad didn't call Linda Erickson himself and Rena said, "Maybe Linda wasn't there." Rena said that Ed said, "The Police are going to be called to Linda's apartment." Rena said that she thought that Ed might have seen the police at Linda's apartment.

Rena said that she then relayed Ed's telephone call to Linda. SA MacLean asked Rena why she thought Ed may have left the area of Linda's apartment when he saw the police. Rena said that because Ed's Camaro was not legal, she thought that he may have left the area.

Rena said that when Ed called Rena again, Ed wanted to know if Rena had called Linda. SA MacLean asked Rena why she thought Ed and Linda were using Rena to relay their telephone messages. Rena said that she had thought about that question when Rena said, "it was almost like using me as a check point."

6. SA Gregory asked Rena what she knew about the abuse of Ada Senenfelder prior to Ada's death. Rena said that she liked Ada and that she thought that the Bolstad's used Ada for her money. Rena said that she once saw Jim Bolstad slap Ada and break Ada's eye glasses because Ada refused to get a beer for Jim Bolstad. Rena said that she thought that the Bolstad's had smashed Ada's bicycle and that Ada told Rena she was scared of the Bolstads.

Murder and Deceit

Status and Appraisal

Rena Bambenek informed special agents if she could be of any further assistance she would be happy to cooperate. The special agents informed her that there was a high probability that they would be in contact with her.

Winona County Law Enforcement Center
Supplementary Report

Name of Complainant
James Erdmanchek 100 Wellborn Road # 44C

Details of offense, progress, of investigation
3-6-92

Writer received call from subj giving his name as James Erdmanchek, wanting to know if the Ada Senenfelder homicide case was still open. Writer told caller that it was. James stated that he had called Sheriff Spitzer a few years ago and told him that he had worked with a subj. in Winona in 1985 who stated that he had killed Ada Senenfelder. James stated that he couldn't remember the guy's name at the time he talked with Spitzer. Writer asked James if he now remember the name. James said that he didn't for sure but for some reason the name "Ringler" comes to mind. James claimed he worked with this subj, at Org. James worked in the rear of the bldg. on water hydrants and this subj worked in the knitting area. James said that he didn't know where this subj lived or his first name or any nicknames he may have had. Just that the name "Ringler" keeps coming to mind. James claimed that this subj had black hair, was dark complected with tannish or light olive skin. James said that this subj made the statement about killing Ada while they were waiting by Lake Winona. As James couldn't recall anything about the subj. writer asked James for his address and phone number. James said he didn't have a phone number but could be contacted by the manager of the Ashley Arms where he lives.

The Letters

A side-story to this human tragedy is the friendship that developed between Jack and I. I never expected to become pen pals with a stranger, much less someone serving a life sentence for murder. My initial impression of Jack came from the newspapers. Even when Kristal talked to me about him it was usually about the case. I came to know and like him on my own. I saw nothing in common and had little interest in finding out who he was. I became interested in the case itself with realizing this story involved real people with families. There was nothing in the newspapers or police interviews telling who Jack was. I got no sense of him at all.

As we started writing letters, we both found it very easy to open up and trust each other. As a writer I am supposed to be good with a sentence, but this was hard to explain to my family, my friends. Only John Jr. got to meet Jack, and through letters and visits we formed a friendship. I expect Jack to like me because I was convinced he was innocent and was trying to get his conviction overturned. I didn't have those thoughts very long. A good deal of what we wrote about was our lives. Jack told me early on that he didn't expect to released, and thought he would die in prison. I discounted those statements, and brushed aside my concerns. He was grateful I wanted to tell his story. I never felt pushed by him laying his life on my shoulders. I never felt anger or any kind of revenge he sought. He told me he would send his grandchildren packages of Kool-aid, and how he worried about me, and how telling his story was taking a toll on me.

During one of my meltdowns he told me to quit, that I had done enough. He wrote me how much he loved racing and how he loved to feel that thrill he always received. Jack spoke of how much he loved his family and friends. Early on, I was exposed to the large group of friends this man had. They are a loyal bunch of friends that have never doubted the man was innocent. Many of them joined me in this fight. Two who were the most passionate were

Scott Schlink and Derek Sutton. They never missed a chance to comment on the blog or to encourage me to keep going. I stayed with Scott on my second trip to Minnesota and became inspired by his devotion to Jack. Scott worked to create the Facebook page for Jack and cooked at the fundraiser for Jack. Jack inspires this type of passion. When I first met Jack, I described him as a gentle giant, one who is intelligent, kind, and soft spoken. He listens carefully to what you say and is very easy to talk to. No matter what kind of day I am having, one of his letters always cheers me up. I saved all of them and go back to see what he wrote. He never takes me for granted or has been negative. He is my friend.

CRIME SCENE NOTES

Michael J. O Gorman

Ref Death of Ada Frances Senenfelder DOB -10-28-44

Location of incident: 566 E. 4th Street Winona., Minnesota
Notified at St. Paul at approximately 2 p.m. Driving time to
Winona, approximately 2 ½ hours.

The residence is located facing 4th Street. The front of the
residence faces in a southerly direction. The front of the house is
offset from the curb area approximately 30 feet, and within that 30
feet there is a concrete sidewalk running east and west. There is a
concrete ramp of approximately 4 ½ feet in front of the house
with a set of concrete steps leading up to a front door. The front
door is located on the southeasterly corner of the building. The
building's primary construction is brick that has been painted white
in color. It has a wooden roof, with shingles. There is a small alcove
over the front door which is also covered with shingles, and the
primary color is green. The exterior door is an aluminum all-
weather style combination door, having no screen in either top or
bottom panel, but glass, intact, in both upper and bottom panels.
The interior door is a hollow core of wooden door. Affixed to that
door is a paper sign, bearing the name, "please use side door." And
several small children's characterized stick-ons at the bottom.
There are two windows that face the street. Both are framed-in
aluminum combination windows. Both appear to be intact. As you
face the front of the house, the window on the far left has a white
opaque substance drooling down on it from the upper right-hand
corner. It appears that possibly at one time the window may have
received and egg strike. On the west side of the residence there is a
walkway of approximately 5 feet, which extends from the front of
the house to the back rear-most portion of the house. Where there

is a wovenwire fence that is in place. The construction of the west side of the house is the same as in the front, that being brick, except for the last approximately 20 –some feet which appears to be an add-on addition, and that is constructed of wood. Within the brick structure there are two more windows on the west side, both of which have aluminum combination windows on them. Both combination windows are intact and show no sign of damage. There is a third, small, approximately 2-foot wide by 4 ½ foot high, aluminum combination window that appears to be leading into the back add-on wooden portion. It's windows are somewhat ajar on the bottom, not of sufficient magnitude to allow entry. There is a wooden casement-framed window on the inside and it is currently in the down closed position. All glass is intact in all of those windows. On the east side of the residence, again a walkway is in place, consisting of a concrete slab walk, bounded on either side by a short strip of grass on the west, or a neighbors side, and a group of what appear to be hacked-off or mowed flowers on the victims side of the sidewalk. Again the building up to the kitchen door, which will be described later, is brick in construction and is painted white as a primary color. There are three windows on the east side. All Three windows contain aluminum casement framing. All glass is intact. No signs of forcible entry are noted. There is a crack, which appears to be old in the lower pane of the third or farthest window from the street on the west side. It runs at an approximately 45 degree angle from the upper left hand side of the window. Said crack, again appears to be old. There is no indication the window has been tampered with or pried on at the bottom or at the sides. The kitchen door is located three-fourths of the way through the east wall. It is in what appears, again to be the added on portion of the residence, at some period of time. Its construction is of wood. It is wood sided, along with slate tile sliding, which runs the remainder of the length of the building. In the porch area there is a kitchen door and a small wooden-framed window which has an air condition, all weather storm door, with both screen and glass intact. There is not damage to glass whatsoever. There is a small hole in the screen, approximately 1 inch long by ½ inch in diameter, which appears to be old in nature. The door has a mechanism can secure itself. The interior kitchen door is constructed of primarily wood, with two glass inserts. Both glass inserts are in good condition, showing no cracks whatsoever. The door has to methods of locking, one being a deadbolt and the other spring latch, which is somewhat vintage, but appears to be operable. The second is a sliding deadbolt about midway down the door. The doorknob mechanism does not show any locking device currently intact. The striker plates are secure in the door casement frames. No screws or signs of force are showing. Continuing down the exterior wall there is one aluminum combination storm window on the west side, again in the added on portion or wooden portion of the structure. It is aluminum combination with screen in place. The screen is shown to be somewhat ajar in the casement itself but no signs of forced entry. There is a wooden window or storm window on the interior portion of the house that is in the down position, and again, no indications of entry through that location. Coming around to the North end of he building there is a small porch affixed to the north end of the building. The porch, for all practical purposes, is an open type of shelter. It has a roof of shingles. It is constructed of wood. There is a wooden screen door outside of a door entering into a room just off from the kitchen. This wooden screen door is standing ajar at the present time. It does show some signs of damage, however, we are unable to determine whether or not it is fresh in nature at this time. There is a hook eye latch on the inside. Said hook eye latch is not in the locked position. It shows no signs of force. There is wooden entry door going into the room from the south. Said entry door has extensive damage just to the right of the doorknob area. It appears to be a hollow core door. The hole is approximately 12-14 inches in length and 4 inches in width, consistent with possibly a shoe, or someone kicking at the door. It appears to be old in nature, as there has been an attempt made by persons unknown to use ½ inch masking tape, many layers of it, to at least weather proof the hole close. Said tape appears to be old and drying out. There is a small doghouse off the porch on the north side of the residence. No animal is seen, nor has been seen by investigators or lab people at this time. Directly behind the house is a spruce tree. There is a building located directly behind the house that is approximately 20X15 or so feet. It is a rather tall structure. It is probably 15-17 feet in height. It has a flat slanted roof. There is a set of wooded stairs leading up the north side of the face of the building to the door where a padlock is affixed. There is a pull –type handle and padlock Again, the padlock is secured. Also on the north side of that building is a second wooden door at ground level, the wooden door is secured by means of a hasp and padlock. There is no indication of what may lay within, either than possibly a storage shed. There is a quantity of broken glass located directly outside the door. The source of this is unknown. No windows are on the east side of this structure. No windows are on the North side, but there is a garage-type, fold up, wooded door therein at ground level. No windows or openings are on the east side of the structure.

There are six rooms on the inside of the house, we'll describe them from the north side of the structure to the sound end. Starting at the north end of the structure. We have a room approximately 15X15, inside that room on the north wall, located in the center is a door leading outside. It is a hollow core wooden door. Again having been described from the outside as having the footprint or kicking impression, with severe damage alongside the knob. It should be noted on the inside an attempt has been made to close this gaping hole, again using masking tape.

Murder and Deceit

The hole does appear to be old in nature. Running from east to west along the north wall, in the east corner, is a chest type deep freeze. Directly adjacent to that, between the freezer and the door, is a small what appears to be, table with a white formica top on it. Just past the door, in a small, alcove, is a washer and dryer. Placed upon that is a box of tide laundry detergent, some miscellaneous clothing, and a bag containing shoes and other assorted clothing. On the floor there is what appears to be a pair of blue trousers, From the northeast corner, along the wall toward the south of this room there is a single bed covered with a red blanket. It has a pillow on it, it is made. It has not been disturbed. There is a window, again directly over the bed, with a curtain over it. All materials appear to be intact and have not been disturbed. There is a wall type gas furnace directly at the south end of the bed. Filling out the rest of the wall is a white, painted cabinet. Across the wall of this room there is a second single bed. It is covered with a blanket type covering and it is fully made and not disturbed. Both beds would be comparable for having children sleep in them. There is a small closet in this room with boxes, hangers and bedding. There is a chest of drawers in the little closet, consisting of six drawers, four being large two being small. The closet itself locks very neat and well. There is a 10 speed girl's bike parked in this room, along the west wall as well as a collapsible miniature game pool table. The room appears to not have had any amount of traffic. On the north wall of the kitchen nothing is found except a walk through doorway, at 110 volt smoke alarm, and a picture or a snowman hanging just to the left of the doorway. Northwest corner is a Frigidaire, Model 205, refrigerator freezer, white porcelain in color. On top of that appliance there is number of boxes of dried milk and food stuff, as well as clock radio. Proceeding north on the west wall we have a four burner gas range and oven. Hanging directly over the top of that is a knife set, brand name Cutco. There are two knife racks, The one on the right appears to be full of utensils. The one on the left is missing what appears to be a knife with a relatively long glade, as well as a second knife with a shorter blade. Moving along to the south, again on the same wall, we find a window, wooded encasement on the interior. There is a portable cupboard in front of it. The window is closed and does not appear to have been tampered with. If it had, no one would have been able to enter, due to the cupboard.

There is a counter space running from the corner in an east west direction. On that counter is a microwave oven, brand name Kenmore. It is at a rather odd angle for usage, and is not plugged in. On top of that are several folded wash clothes and a cookbook. Directly adjacent to the microwave oven is a Norelco dial-a-brew coffee pot. It is in the on position. There are approximately 8-10 cups of coffee in it. The coffee is warm and looks like it has been brewing for quite some time. Initial officers the scene state proceeding along the same cupboard. We come to the sink. It is a two compartment, porcelain sink. In the right hand corner it has a drain holder. There are two cups which appear to have been used recently. Both have fluid in them. One fluid is relatively clear and the second is dark and appears to be coffee. There is a large glass bowl in the center of the sink. Inside of that is a smaller plastic bowl. Both bowls are filled with brown murky fluid and a single plate Is also in the sink, it does not appear to have been washed. There is a small glass just adjacent to the sink at the top, sitting on the cupboard. There is also a bottle of Palmolive dish soap sitting on top of the cupboard adjacent to the sink. There are wooden cupboards on this wall over the top of the counter, consisting of two rather large cup board on this wall over the top of the counter, consisting of two rather large cupboards and two rather small ones directly above the sink. In the center of the room is a kitchen table with a metal legs and white or off white to gray formica top. On the top of that table are two packages of hamburger buns. Both packages are new. There have been no buns removed from either package. There is a package of what appears to be sliced ham purchased from a meat department, or possibly a meat market. The package is standing open on the top of the table and there are two stacks of ham showing. Initial reports state that the ham, earlier was cool to the touch. It is now warming and fluid is draining off of it. From all outward appearance, it would seem that someone was going to make a sandwich or several. Proceeding further south in the structure we come to a small, approximately 4 foot hall said hallway eventually opens up into what appears to be the living room portion of the residence. Just prior to opening up into that room, we come upon a small, maybe 5x5 room, which is a bathroom. Over the top of the shower stall, which is as you come in, are a series of what appears to be both to where nothing is along the wall until we come up to the sink area and on the sink is a can of snoopy pump style soap. There is a kitchen bathroom medicine cabinet. On top of that are several bottles of shampoo and air freshener, as well as spray deodorant and a cup of toothbrushes. Underneath the pedestal that the sink is on is assorted bar soap, scouring powders, different sprays another tube of snoopy hand soap, and the normal products that you would find in a bathroom for either cleaning the bathroom or supply storage. There is also an access port into the cellar portion of the residence from this location. It was examined by the laboratory staff. Access to it was very difficult it required the use of several pry tools, once down in the basement, nothing of remarkable value was noted and it does not appear that the room has been entered for quite some time. Proceeding to the next room, that being a room we will describe as the living room we will start from the northwest coroner and work down the west wall. Located at about a 45 deg angle a Magnavox color television set with rabbit ears affixed, however it does appear that there is cable TV hooked up to the set. The set was found in the "On" position at the time the initial officers arrived. Directly below the television set there is a second shelf. That shelf contains approximately three, either paintings or pictures. All appear to be rather old and it does not appear that the cabinet has been opened in sometime. Proceeding down the wall to the south, we find a clock bearing a photograph of a deer in a wooded scene. The clock is operable. It is battery operated, as no power cord is showing. A window is located in mid-wall. It is wood casement window on the inside aluminum casement on the outside. The window is in the down position. The glass is secure. There is a pane that looks to be newly replaced however as it is still bears the glass sticker on the outside. There are cobwebs across the bottom of the interior of the window and they do not appear to be broken. There appears to be no entry through that window. The window is covered by a sheer blue curtain with a white flower design on it. The remainder of the wall is unremarkable, except the folded card table which is in the south corner of that wall. Coming from the southwest corner of that room and working our way to the est. Along the east wall, is a sofa. Said sofa is rather old. It has a blanket and comforter laying on it, as well as two pillows with white pillow cases, which are somewhat soiled. The comforter is positioned in such a way as it appears to have been laid on at one point in time. Someone may have been covered with the remaining half of it. There are a pair of tennis shoes sitting directly at the head of the couch, or where the head pillows are. They are velcro fastener type tennis shoes. Primary color is gray. They have white stripes on the sides of them. Going to the gas on the same wall is a in wall gas heater, brand name, Tempco. The heater is shared between this room and the room directly adjacent to the living room, that being the room where the deceased is lying, or the front bedroom. Directly adjacent to the east of this in wall heater is a door leading to the front bedroom. In the southeast corner of this room there is a 3 shelf knick-knack shelf with assorted knick knacks, There is a pair of shoes in the southeast corner. Working our way back north on the east wall is a window with sheer blue curtains affixed thereto and they do have a reddish brown stain on them The interior window is a wooden casement. It is found in the down condition, the glass is secure. There are cobwebs across the bottom of the window and they are not disturbed. Located directly in front of that window is a two tier small TV style coffee table with porcelain lamp sitting thereon. Said lamp is electric and is plugged in it is not operating at this time. Proceeding again north along this same wall there is a picture of a female, hanging approximately 6-6 ½ feet up on the wall. It shows the female having shorter brown hair. Directly underneath that picture is what appears to be a closet. Without opening it, we are unable to determine whatever it is a closet. It appears to be some sort of a storage closet. Its size is approximately 4 by 2 feet deep and 5 feet high. Atop that box is a series of what appears to be children's games, misc children's articles etc. Directly adjacent and approximately half of which lies right behind this previously described box is a second window on this wall. Said window is a wooden casement on the inside. It is also covered by sheer blue curtain material. There are cobwebs on the inside. It is also covered by sheer blue curtain material. All glass is intact in the window. In front of this window also is a light brown naugahyde-covered chair, in that chair are two fairly thin pillows. A string-art boat hangs from the wall. Working from the northeast corner of this room to the west, along the shelves, all of which are completely full of misc knick knacks. There is also an ashtray with contents which appear to be several marijuana roaches. There is also a card and an envelope entitled, Happy Valentines day mom. Nothing appears to be all that much amiss here. On the wall directly to the west of this knick knack shelf are several art crafts which appear to have been drawn by a younger child. The next thing we come to is again, a chest of drawers consisting of four drawers. The only one of the drawers is ajar is the top one. Atop of this article it is covered with a towel. There is some newspaper a single letter another string art ship, some seashells and a comb, a pen a rather old gas wick lamp and what appears to be two jar style candles. Directly underneath the chest of drawers is a white plastic bag. The contents of this bag are unknown at this time. Nothing is really remarkable about the ceiling in this room either other than there is a fluorescent light located directly in the center of it recessed lighting in the ceiling. There is a smoke alarm over the door on the south wall that leads to the room where the deceased body was located.

Description of the room where the assault occurred.

We will start from the doorway leading from the living room portion into this room. We will work on the north wall of this room from its northeasterly corner toward the west. From the northwest corner to the walk through door opening, entering this room, there is nothing on the wall. The doorway leading into the room does not have a door. It is wide open doorway. Directly to the west of the door is a light switch, which operates the fluorescent light recessed in the ceilings. Directly adjacent to the switch is the other half of the in-wall room heater as been described earlier in the living room. Proceeding westerly along that same wall we come to a rather spacious closet which has no doors on it. On that bar is a series of what appears to be snowmobile suits and other misc. winter clothing. The clothing appears to be female in nature, of such sizes that would fit children. Located under that clothing is a series of children's play toys, a three drawer chest of drawers all painted pink. There are several children's suitcases on the floor. Directly outside of that closet are two canister-type vacuum cleaners and attachments. That takes us up to the northwest corner of this room and we will now proceed in a southerly directly along the west wall. Along that west wall is a single bed which has a white and multicolored print bedspread on it. The bed is a made condition. It has a pillow at its head. It has several children dolls on

Murder and Deceit

it and the print on the bedspread would be consistent with that of a child's. Directly over the bed on the wall is a picture of Christ and two small children. The front wall of the house or the southern most wall and going east has two windows in it. The first of which is a wooden casement design. All of the glass is in it's place. The windows are somewhat narrow and rather tall in nature. Between windows is again string art, design of a sailboat. In the center of the wall and extending into the center of the room is a double bed with headboard. There is dust on the headboard. In the center of the bedspread is a stained area which is dark red to nearly dark brown, consisting of four major stains, with several other minor smaller type stains directly in the same area. The stained area is an approximate 6-7 inches in length and 3-4 inches in width. Again, the bed is made. It does not appear to have slept in or have been used. There are two pillow on the bed that are covered by the bedspread at the time of the dictation. The bed will have been taken apart for examination. Located directly to the east of the bed is a lamp and stand. And as part of that stand there is a shelf. Its primary construction is metal. It is cream-colored lampshade on it. There are a series of blood spatters on the exterior of the lamp shade. The stains do not continue or at least they are not readily noticeable away from a direct line site to the body. There is a photograph of a small female child, framed, hanging above said lamp. There is also a double gang light switch box directly to the left of the lamp, between the lamp and the door. These switches upon arrival are both found in the off position. Both switches do function. The front door is hollow core in nature, leads to the outside or south side of the residence. There is remaining 12-14 inches of wall space into the corner. This would be the south and east corner, on which nothing is hanging. Starting from the southeast corner, on which nothing is hanging. The window is covered by the same print curtains as cover the other two windows in the room, that print being a red flower over white background.

Lying directly in front of this window is a single bed. It is a brown frame. The bed frame is out from the wall approximately 10 inches. It is out from the head and approximately the same distance.

On top of the bed is what appears to be, at this time, the fully-clothed body of the white female. The body has a pair of blue jeans on, which are currently secured by a brown leather belt with white trim. I am unable to determine whether the belt is attached or unbuckled. From what I can see, the zipper of the pants appears to be in an up position. The top half of the the body, from what is visible at this time is a clad in a pink kind of frizzy, short sleeved pullover blouse with a waistband, elastic in nature. The feet are, for all practical purposes, covered by the bedspread and it appears that the foot is clothed with a dark stocking. The body is approximately one half to two thirds off the bed and the upper torso area from the waist toward the face exposed, with the left side being concealed by the wall. The right arm extends downward from the shoulder, along the side of the body to the elbow, the arm is bent in an upward 45 deg angle, back toward the breast. The hand rests at the window ledge. Visible on the hand is a wound to the top part of the thumb, between the first knuckle and second and third it appears to be a deep wound. The left shoulder is not visible. The left arm proceeds at a 90 deg angle from the floor to the ceiling, from the shoulder up to the elbow. The arm currently rests on the bottom of the chin. At the elbow, it again takes an approximately 90 deg bend, and extends across the full chest area of the body and in fact, the hand is past the right shoulder, about up to the wrist with the hand extending on the bed. Resting in a parallel nature to the body on the outside portion of the left wrist, is the blade of a rather large what appears to be butcher knife. Said butcher knife has a blood stain on its tip to all but approximately 1½ inch of the blade. The overall length of the blade appears to be 8 inches or more. The knife has a wooden handle with brass rivets in it. It resembles the same style of the knives found in the kitchen and previously described. Half of the window curtain is entangled in the knife handle and lies on top of the right arm. Said curtain is twisted several times and does appear to be blood stained. The body is laying upon this off-white or light blue nobby bedspread. The bedspread is folded across the lower portion of the body from the right knee on down, totally covering the lower right leg and extends across the left foot from just under the knee almost a full extremity of the body. It extends off the bed. The bedspread then opens up almost to an area encompassing the remaining upper surface of the bed. It extends off the bed on the left side and presumably lies underneath the body onto the floor. There is a single pillow at the head of the bed, which has a white and blue star striped design on the pillowcase. Underneath the body and onto the floor, there is a quantity of blood that extends from an area directly from the head down to approximately the waist up on the window and in the window ledge. This is a splatter design. The way the bed material is situated is not indicative of a large struggle before her attacker would have been noticed. In fact, there is nothing to suggest a struggle premortem. From the bed of from the window on the left side of the window, it appears what possibly could be construed as a finger impression blood stain. There are numerous blood spatters just to the left of the window, extending to a chest of drawers which is located right at the head of the bed, a distance of approximately 1 foot. They extend upward from the floor approx. 3 ½ ft The blood spatter expert will have some other qualifying statements about those. Filling out the remainder of the wall to the north is a formica covered six drawer chest of drawers. having a mirrored back to it. There is a child's bank, several cassette music tapes and a statue of a small deer. There is a black pair for horn rimmed glasses laying directly dead center in the middle of the chest. There is what appears to be Kleenex, or tissue anyway crumbled-up laying adjacent to the glasses and extending either from that tissue or from underneath it at least is a series of curled hair, a cassette recorder. There is also a statue of a small bunny rabbit behind that. On top of the tape player recorder is a microphone and an eyeglass case with a pocket clip. There is a photograph, it depicts give children. The floor of the room is remarkably clean. There are no clothes or misc debris scattered about it. The celling is a white, suspended style fluorescent light. Said light is operable. We should note that the volume on the television is consistent with very easy listening from inside of the living room portion.

Decide For Yourself

In the cold winter of 2003–2004 in Denver, Colorado. I met Michael Moore, the filmmaker at a book signing. Prior to the signing he spoke for over two hours. One of the points he made was an extensive exercise with the audience. The venue was at the University of Denver, where my son Matt graduated, and home to a top-notch hockey team. This sport attracts a large group of students who are from Canada. He asked for volunteers from the audience and assembled three from the USA and three from Canada. He asked them to name the President and Vice President of the USA, and the governor of Colorado. They answered in order George Bush, Dick Cheney, and Bill Owens. The three Americans were all female and said they were on the Dean's list. They were asked to name the prime minister, deputy PM or a single governor in Canada. Stumped and embarrassed, they sat down. Around this same time I read in *Newsweek* that 31% of a group of fifth graders, given 20 minutes to find Iraq on a world atlas, couldn't. I went home with a thought—actually a lot of thoughts.

Americans think they are the center of the universe. We have lost our edge in much of country by lack of curiosity and our ability to think and challenge what we are told. Most, if not all of our information comes from television whose news channels are owned by a handful of people. After the event the University of Denver, I began to read news from outside of the US online. It was surprisingly different. I learned different perspectives from the same story. We are so polarized as a country; we learn to accept the judgment of others. We have come to accept corruption and tragedy as normal, and are more easily upset over getting cut off in traffic or having to wait in line for a little while then to be moved by injustice.

My hope for this book is twofold: I hope this proves Jack Nissalke is innocent and was framed for the murder of Ada

Senenfelder by corrupt public officials. Second, I hope it forces you, as a reader, to make up your own mind about the people and things around you. Let us stop allowing others to think for us.

The Appeals Process

The word appeal has several meanings one of them which means to ask a higher court to reverse the decisions of a lower court. When the jury convicted Jack in less than four hours of deliberation, he received an automatic life sentence, which also guarantees an automatic appeal. Hundreds of time I've been asked to present the massive amount of evidence I possess that indicates Jacks innocence to a court. It just doesn't work that way. At the time of this writing, Jack is mostly locked down in his narrow cell in Rush City, Minnesota. His court appointed lawyer has stood in front of the state Supreme Court as the justices had Jack's reasons for appeal there. Tom Gort, recalled from his new position, stood up for Winona county as they took turns giving their positions. The only things that can be presented here are possible irregularities in Jack's trial, making the point that he didn't get a fair trial. No new evidence can be presented here. Even if somebody stood up and confessed to killing Ada, the judge wouldn't allow this at this time.

Does that make any sense at all? Well, they do get to hear how the judge went into the jury several times to tamper with them during deliberations—and how no possible theory other than Jack killing Ada was allowed in the courtroom. We can only hope they say yes, as the MSSC rarely ever grants one. If they do, Winona County has the choice to retry his appeal. Jack can bring up more irregularities to them over a long and expensive legal battle as he grows older and older. As this point, Jack's spirit is strong and the will to not give up is intact. I pray it stays strong.

JACK DID NOT KILL ADA

1. Alibi: Jack Nissalke was at Linda Parrish's house party the night of the murder. Photographs and witnesses consistently corroborate his story.

2. The real motive: Ed Bolstad had no alibi. He left the party. Police saw him leave when they responded to a loud noise complaint. He was later seen at The Happy Chef, wet and disheveled. He had coffee and made and received calls from Rena, wondering why the cops were at Linda's. He would show scratches, bloody clothes, and a cleaned out car. Ed's motive was a revenge from Jim, his brother. Rena was probably involved over Ed and Ada having sex. Experts point to a woman, as 33 wounds mostly shallow, looks like a crime of passion.

3. DNA: Blood evidence went missing and the only surviving DNA evidence came from a cigarette butt that matched only 5 of 17 points of Nissalke's DNA. It was not a reasonable match—and this particular DNA test (Y-STR) is useful only in sexual assault crimes.

4. Reward: The $50,000 reward offered in 2006 produced three women who decided to recant their testimony twenty years prior and tell a new story blaming Nissalke. Their rehearsed story was revealed to be inconsistent and full of holes in court. The reward money for Senenfelder's murder remains unclaimed.

5. Jury: The jury, which included a convicted murderer, was tampered with by the media and the judge. The jury spent fewer than three hours deliberating over 10,000 pages of testimony and evidence.

Acknowledgments

I wish to thank the following people for helping me with Jack's story: Ron Nissalke, Bonnie Nissalke, Laurie Nissalke, Kristal Nissalke, Julie Nissalke, Corey Prolo, Cody Prolo, Harley Howell, John Senenfelder, Scott Schlink, Derek Sutton, Tasha Welch, Cynthia Aragon, Craig Holm, Linda Parrish, Rollie Beeman, Mike Gierok, Sarah Elmquist, Edina Rush, The Winona Public Library, The Acoustic Cafe, and Bubs Bar.

CPSIA information can be obtained
at www.ICGtesting.com
Printed in the USA
LVHW030004110323
741360LV00004B/498